T0326038

VIA YPRES

VIA YPRES

Story of the
39th Divisional Field Ambulances

BY

ALLAN JOBSON
(72109. Private, R.A.M.C.)

With a Foreword by
General SIR HUBERT DE LA POER GOUGH
G.C.M.G., K.C.B., K.C.V.O., etc.

UNIFORM

UNIFORM

First published by The Westminster City Publishing Company in 1934.
This edition first published by Uniform in 2017
an imprint of Unicorn Publishing Group

Unicorn Publishing Group
101 Wardour Street
London W1F 0UG
www.unicornpublishing.org

All rights reserved. Without limiting the rights under copyright reserved, no part of
this publication may be reproduced, stored in or introduced into a retrieval system
or transmitted in any form or by any means (electronic, mechanical photocopying,
recording or otherwise) without the prior written permission of both the copyright
owner and the above publisher of this book.

Copyright © Unicorn Publishing Group, 2017

A catalogue record for this book is available from the British Library

ISBN 978-1-910500-21-7

Printed and bound in Great Britain

Please note: *In producing in facsimile from original historical documents, any
imperfections may be reproduced and the quality may be lower than modern
typesetting or cartographic standards.*

DEDICATED

*" To my comrades; and the memory
of those, who in the corners of a
foreign field remain forever England."*

VIA YPRES

Story of the
39th Divisional Field Ambulances

BY

ALLAN JOBSON
(72109. Private, R.A.M.C.)

With a Foreword by
General Sir Hubert de la Poer Gough
G.C.M.G., K.C.B., K.C.V.O., etc.

1934
The Westminster City Publishing Company Ltd.
94, Clapham Park Road
London, S.W. 4

Photo)   *(J. Russell & Sons*

COLONEL G. W. BRAZIER-CREAGH, C.B., C.M.G.
A.D.M.S. 39TH DIVISION

TABLE OF CONTENTS

Foreword

HUNDREDS of such books as this, in many languages, have been written by those who took part in the Great War, but yet are there too many? Can anyone take up this book and read its pages without being profoundly moved? Very few will be able to do so without feeling a lump rising in the throat, without feeling a great surge of pride and affection for the unselfish devotion and heroism of these men whose story is told in these pages, or without a deep pang of sorrow at the tragedy of it all.

Such feelings will be roused more strongly in the English hearts, because everyone can see and must realise the greatness, the splendid yet simple courage and self-sacrifice, and the tender kindness which is to be found in this great people.

The men of this race, going to the War, to take part in the great struggle—mostly mere boys—quite non-militaristic in their education, happy, cheerful, perhaps a bit casual, and yet when confronted with the great task, with all the danger and all the misery and horror, never faltering and remaining cheerful and gallant, but getting down to the root of their job, being thorough, attaining efficiency, and undeterred by the extremes of misery and physical fatigue or the risk of death.

No, I cannot think that too many of such War-books have been written. Here is another, from a slightly new angle perhaps, that of the Medical Service instead of the front-line soldier.

But before reading a dozen pages, the reader will realise that these men also were front-line soldiers, and that the same splendid devotion is found among them as was shown by those who carried out the tasks which fell to the lot of " the common soldier."

HUBERT GOUGH.

London, S.W.10.

PREFACE

———

THANKS are due, and gladly accorded, to all those who have in any way contributed to the making of this book. Especial thanks must be tendered to Brig.-Gen. Sir J. E. Edmonds, C.B., C.M.G., and the staff at Audit House, for their courtesy and kindness in providing free access to the War Diaries, upon which the volume is founded. It should be here noted that the account of the Retreat is based on a report issued by G Branch of the Division, supplemented by that made by the A.D.M.S.

The photographs are the product of illicit cameras, and as such, unique.

It is, perhaps, not of the sin of presumption to say that this account of the Medical Services of the Division is also a history of the Division in outline. A work that has not yet been attempted.

Tribute also must be paid to Col. G. W. Brazier-Creagh, for the use of his papers placed at the writer's disposal, and to Q.M.-Sergeant F.H. Herbert, M.S.M. and Major J. W. Wayte, M.C., without whose fostering care this book could hardly have been born.

A. J.

" The journey of a thousand miles begins with a single step."

CHINESE PROVERB

PROLOGUE

———

THE story of the 39th Divisional Field
Ambulances begins in the year of our Lord
1915 at various recruiting offices, best known
to the novitiates concerned, and continues in a
thin, uncertain stream of variable humanity, finding
its way to a hole in the Sussex Downs, facing the
sea, at Cow Gap, Eastbourne. Here the lines of
white tents, the whitewashed stones, the martial
sounds and atmosphere welcomed the embryo
soldier to the service of his country, and to a fellow-
ship, unique and abiding. From South, North,
West and East came these men with whom we were
to live, eat and sleep. Whom we were destined to
love or tolerate and be amused with or annoyed
by the little peculiarities that went to the making
of the individual, our brother in the ranks. Soon
sun and rain, the splash of the sea and the eternal
parade ground, bronzed these pale faces of shops,
offices and factories into premature veterans. In
three brief years we were to experience all phases
of war and crowd into service the lifetime of old
campaigners.

Upon arrival, the raw material of this fine
friendship was carefully docketted, given a number,
conducted to a tent, provided with blankets and
left to simmer for the night. Thereafter arises in

many minds memories of first meals, the first night's attempt at sleep, the first shave, and, not least, the first visit to the latrines.

First impressions are certainly of great worth and the experiences of the active service that was to come could not obliterate these days that to us were full of revolutions. So foreign, so utterly opposed to all our ways, and yet so fraught with the great education of our manhood. That many look back and thank God for the day they joined and the men they met is a testimony to the truth of the story concerning an ill-wind.

The great Newman in a hymn which was of peculiar efficacy as a lullaby, says " And in the morn those angel faces smile." To us, recruits, incipient soldiers, the angel faces resolved themselves into Sergeant-Majors Lloyd and Cudmore, who awaited us on the sound of " Fall in." Who will forget the marchings to and fro, the fear of it and the dread of it which these old stagers drilled into us. How they shouted and curled the lip, hurled threats and made the knees to shake, wielding a power of which an eastern monarch was as a child. It is recorded that so successful were these two in their efforts that one poor wight was led to hand in a week's notice of termination of contract as he wished to go home. And yet now, Messrs. Lloyd and Cudmore, by whatever fire you warm your hands, we would stroke your beards, recall with pleasure the vigour of your voices and thank you for the job you so faithfully carried out of licking our raw material into shape.

Day followed day across those Sussex hills, crammed with the incidentals of Army routine. " Form fours " was followed by " Quick March," and such intricacies as fatigues, lectures on the hillside by youthful officers, inspection by this man and that, and the incidental calls of " Cook House," completed the round. To say nothing of the hut labelled Y.M.C.A., where we drank tea, wrote letters and sang lustily, " Keep the Home Fires Burning," and " There's a Silver Lining." Those hearty melodies to some were fraught with a catch in the throat. Vaccination, inoculation, obliteration by a sleep deep and welcome. With dreams of Vicarage Road and the Workhouse to complete the details carry on the recruit a stage further until the great and glorious morning when the new uniform was provided by Q.M. Stores. Then the unsuspecting onlooker might have witnessed the doing up of parcels on Eastbourne Station and the despatch home of all the glories attaching to civilian existence. For us, indeed, there was no turning back.

One illuminating parade soon after arrival was that on which we were asked our occupation in civilian life and our religion. Many diverse careers were disclosed in the former answers, and many esoteric cults in the latter. Even the Padres seemed to be influenced by the uniform they wore and their theology ran in military categories. " You cannot be a Peculiar Person," said they, " therefore you must be C. of E."

Life at the Camp became more tolerable as each day passed. The open air, physical jerks and general routine coloured existence with rosier hues and the rough and ready meals began to be looked forward to with eagerness. Those great slices of bread and butter, with a dash of jam, and the pint of tea, went down as food of a daintier variety does not always to-day. To see men scamper up for an early morning cup of coffee before the trot over the Downs, showed that life was a healthy thing.

And with the appetite for what the Cook-house supplied came, too, the humorous outlook on the new life. Who will forget those early morning doubles? The variety of shapes and sizes scattering along in undress uniform, and the names which came readily to fat and thin, winded, and unwinded. We watched, too, the arrival of other recruits, some carrying attache cases containing alarm clocks and pyjamas, and gloated over the discomfort that must be theirs until they could be as old as we in the Service. And when two diverse creatures made their appearance one morning, one much older than the other, they were taken for father and son. "You cruel b——r" was the greeting for the veteran, "you can join if you like, but send the kid home."

One institution in the camp is worthy of mention, viz., the arrival of the mail. To hear, amid the eager crowd surrounding the distributor, one's name called, was music indeed. And one had to wait to the end for letters were not sorted into alphabetical order.

It is, of course, a well-known thing that soldiers may not have long hair. Witness, then, the military hair-cut accomplished in the open-air, on the hillside, seated on a wooden box. How the onlookers, even

those waiting to be shorn, screamed with laughter
as each sentient recruit bore the brunt of the
heartless shears. Poet and peasant emerged alike,
the veriest convicts of their former selves. What
their best girl thought when, later, they returned
home and removed their cap, is not recorded!
We had not been many days at Eastbourne when
we were suddenly formed up one afternoon,
portioned off by the Sergeant-Major, and found,
to our astonishment, that we were constituted into
the three Field Ambulances. By an accident of
position we belonged to 132, 133 or 134 Field
Ambulance.

Each Ambulance was placed under the charge of
a youthful officer: Lieut. O. Swinnerton to 132;
Lieut. S. J. Lindeman to 133; Lieut W. R. Tutt
to 134. Full of years as far as service went, for they
were some six weeks our senior, assisted by N.C.O's
who were our contemporaries in ignorance. Only
for some fragmentary periods were we under the
charge of the regular Sergeant-Majors Lloyd and
Cudmore. The temporary officers appointed
remained in charge until the regular commanders
were appointed some weeks later.

Taking into consideration the little service these
officers had seen, it reflects great credit upon them
that they handled the job so well. To suddenly
find one's self in sole charge of some 200 men,
to arrange billets, select N.C.O's, handle £400
to £500 every few days, personally pay landladies
and do everything else, was no enviable task.

The birth of the Ambulances seemed to disturb the
elements, for as soon as this was accomplished,

the weather broke and we were flooded out of the
tents. Winds blew, and rain fell, until almost
the parade ground itself was washed away. It was
not long before we were escorted to billets in private
houses in the Pevensey Road area of Eastbourne,
and made guests of wondering landladies.

It was from now onwards that we realised our
identity. Our own Orderly Rooms were evolved,
our own duties formed into the perfect round.
Now and again the monotony of training was relieved
by a long route march into the surrounding country;
once or twice, for recruiting purposes, headed by
the depot band of the Royal Sussex Regiment.
How proud we were and how elated when one or
two trophies were marched in. Who more than
ourselves was entitled to sing, " Tipperary " and
the refrain about joining Lord Kitchener's Army:

"Seven bob a week and nothing to eat,
　　Damned great boots and blisters on your feet."

even if we did look a little odd with our blue
overcoats and khaki uniforms. And it was whilst
in billets that we were served out with the pipeclay
belts that required so much spit and polish.

Not long, however, were we destined to be
emasculated by feather beds, early morning tea and
the ministrations of doting landladies. Rumour
began to run and although within sight of a
Christmas dinner in the comfortable kitchens we
were marched away to the station en-route for an
unknown destination. This turned out to be
Twezeldown Camp, Farnham, Surrey.

Many will recall that journey along the South coast, until when Portsmouth was reached, rumour became so powerful that with difficulty we were kept from boarding the troopship for Active Service. However, the train turned soon right and when Winchester appeared our destiny was secure.

We were certainly fortunate in our choice of Twezeldown as a training centre, for it was surely one of the finest camps in the country. Under the charge of Major Stafford, R.A.M.C., everything was provided that an embryo soldier could require. Airy, comfortable huts, lit by electric light, model cook houses, dining rooms, reading room, canteens and bath houses, in which latter we bathed in trays, set in cubicles with open fronts, and presented the appearance to onlookers of a series of naked Buddhas. Post Office, Church, Cinema, bread store and incinerator. What more could one want with the " Horns " Public House but across the parade ground?

We now became acquainted with the ration loaves, round and uniform, which like famous vintages, had to be of a certain age ere they could be issued for consumption.

Built, too, amid the pines of Aldershot, and on sandy soil, the all too frequent rains had but little effect, and left the heavy-footed soldier tolerably clean. Life here was an all too short progress to the embarkation point.

It was here another step was passed in our career, for we were discovered to be a portion of the 39th Division then in training at Witley, Surrey.

Not long after our arrival our new Commanding Officers were appointed and joined us to take charge. Captain A. S. Littlejohn to 132; Captain A. Scott-Williams, who had been a prisoner of war in Germany and an inmate of the terrible typhus camp at Ruhleben, to 133; and Captain V. C. Honeybourn to 134. Other officers, amongst whom the maple leaf was much in evidence, had by now made their appearance and within a few days we were at full strength, including the Quarter-Master.

Now, too, the Horse Transport Section of the A.S.C. arrived with their gifts of eternal youth in the shape of horsed ambulances, G.S. wagons, limbers and water cart. Who will forget this legacy of abiding fatigue, the impedimenta that required as much attention as the child that refuses to grow up. These precious " Marks " of varying numerical strength needed constant guards, while the wheels thereof and the metal portions gave room for sundry cursings. One wonders sometimes at the military mind which equipped units for service in France with establishments as used in the South African War. The one was as much like the other as Wimbledon is to the homely table tennis, and the horsed ambulances or hirdey girdeys as they were facetiously called, were as useful in France as a headache to a healthy man.

Whilst on the subject of equipment we should mention that the contents of the G.S. wagons arrived too, with their panniers and loads. Then were the troops busy, loading and unloading *ad nauseam*, until the intricate work was as child's play.

Meanwhile we trained. Trod firmly the racecourse that adjoined our lines and avoided the bogs that strewed the heath. Went route marches into the unspoiled ways of Surrey and Hampshire. Were sometimes lost by the officer our guide, and returned to camp late for the great meal. Had whole Field Days when we mimicked war. Dug various useful offices in the innocent heath and learnt the value of shovel and pick. Sometimes a night march relieved the monotony, when no sound was permitted but the shuffle of marching feet. Hilarity returned, however, when coffee and biscuits appeared in the mess room.

Our first Christmas came and went, leaving behind an array of greasy plates and a sense of fullness not always known after eating. Some became slightly overcome by the good things freely supplied, and amused their fellows by the flow of wit thus unlocked. Who could forget the sight of a tall, gaunt Welshman with stentorious voice, and a Scotch companion who insisted on marching up and down, between the beds, attired only in shirts, carrying the dry scrubbers at the slope and singing "A wee doc an' doris, a wee drap, that's arl."

It was at Twezeldown that we first met, in a sudden descent, the Colonel whose acquaintance we were more fully to appreciate as time progressed. He came, like the Roman of old, he saw, and what he

saw made his head to vibrate and the wonderful
posteen coat he wore to almost turn colour. He
cursed, but, fortunately, it was only the officers
he cursed, and then departed. Some said he was
the A.D.M.S., but what that was no one knew.
He certainly left us much room for speculation.
Whilst here, too, we qualified for Corps pay, by
passing examinations in certain branches of medical
knowledge of the "first aid" variety. This was
accompanied by the inevitable howlers, as, for
example, the man who when asked where his
patella was assured one of the examiners that he
had never been served out with such a thing.

The stay at Haig Hutments was relieved by an
occasional "pass." First came Christmas with its
few days interlude, and then but a short while after
the final leave before we embarked. These were
acceptable and pleasant hours that concluded all
too swiftly.

At the beginning of March, 1916, having been at
the camp some three months, we formed up and amid
the strains of the "Conquering Hero" supplied
by the depot band, marched a long and wandering
way to Farnborough Station where we entrained for
Southampton. A happy, clean, wholesome collection
of irresponsible lads, whom, amid the weeks of
camp life, had grown to know each other well and
appreciate the worth of the other fellow's character.
A farewell dinner was given the previous evening
to the officers of our units by the officers who were
not yet proceeding overseas. This was a somewhat
hectic evening and there was some shattering of

glasses. Thick heads and mixed memories greeted the morning.

At Southampton, when night fell, amid twinkling lights, we crossed in three various troopships. The 132nd in the " City of Benares," known to thousands of soldiers as the " Ghost Ship "; the 133rd in the " Australind "; and the 134th in the " Glenarn Head " to greet the morning and the coast of France at the port of Le Havre.

An uncertain world awaited us.

" Our greatest happiness was now to be useful to the sufferers . . .

But, good God, what a battle it was, and if it should not be the conclusion: and as long as Bonaparte is in France I cannot persuade myself it can be . . . but I must not write politics ! "
July 9, 1815.

THE CREEVEY PAPERS

LA BASSEE

DAYBREAK found us swung to, in bitterly cold and snowy weather, at the entrance to Le Havre harbour. After some delay we slowly moved to our place at the quayside, passing a submerged vessel at the mouth of the narrow channel. Now was everyone an eager and interested spectator of unfamiliar and novel scenes. A new country of quaint and untrodden ways. The buildings attracted us with their shuttered windows and rambling roofs; and the crowded quays and boulevards, full of bustling life, held out prospects of much sightseeing.

It was sometime before we disembarked and then were fatigues in evidence, assisting to unload wagons, G.S. and limber, and all the stores we carried, not forgetting the horses and mules. This done we lined up, and over the cobbled streets, worn by the feet of many troops, marched away through the fascinating town to the hills above, that clustered round the old sea port. We were en-route for a rest camp, which after some effort was reached. This proved to be a collection of tents secreted in the corner of a field half-hidden in snow. It is no exaggeration to say the snow was twelve inches deep! What a welcome and how we almost wished ourselves back at Twezeldown! Some discovered the washing troughs and abluted amid the wintry scene. Some found a crowded Y.M.C.A. hut, the air of which could be cut with a knife. While everyone discovered, under the snow, one of the most comfortable night's rest they had ever had. As snug as any hibernating creature. The camp was generally voted the next morning not such a bad place after all, and we were to know many worse.

A hurried, though appreciated breakfast and we were marching to the train. We hardly expected first-class coaches, neither did we anticipate the trucks we did find, labelled Hommes 40, Chevaux 8; but with the unceremonious fashion to which we were now accustomed we were bundled in. As we appeared to be considerably more than eight in a truck we concluded we did not come under the category of Chevaux.

But who can forget that journey? Rumbling on and on. Now towards Paris, now away. Through flat agricultural country of Normandy, past hamlets clustering about the tapering Church, through this town and that. Evening came and still we journeyed amid snow and shadow, watching, until eyes could trace no longer, the slender trees with tufted tops or the crude, mysterious outlines of many buildings set against a wintry sky. But still the engine shrilly whistled and still we rumbled on.

The night was passed in fitful sleeping, for there was hardly room in which to stretch out one's legs, whilst the intense cold came in through the cracks of floor and door and stiffened our aching limbs. The faint light of a lantern suspended from the roof of the trucks was barely sufficient to light the forms of the restless sleepers on the floor below. The officers were accommodated in ordinary carriages, but it is questionable if they were better off for we could at times stretch our limbs. Before dawn we found ourselves at St. Omer.

Here surely was a place the name of which sounded familiar, for was it not the headquarters of the British Armies in France and Flanders? And had not Lord Roberts died here? But we were not destined for St. Omer and on we rumbled until Hazebrouck was reached. It was from the local stations of this district that we detrained. The 132nd and the 134th Field Ambulances at Thiennes and the 133rd Field Ambulance at Steenbecque. Here the officers received the famous Hazebrouck 5A map, with which they were to become so familiar, and omlettes of unfading memory.

Now was much excitement. Staff Officers were here to meet us, and not only ourselves but our impedimenta had to be got off the train that had taken so long to bring us a comparatively short journey. Snow was still falling and bitter winds howling across the wintry waste. One ambulance dumped their packs by the roadside while they assisted unloading the stores and when they returned to their possessions had the utmost difficulty in sorting out their belongings which had become hidden under the snow. One incident should be recalled of a man who had lost his boots during the long train journey and was faced with a march in carpet slippers. He had to be accommodated in one of the horsed ambulances—the first casualty. Unloading having been completed we fell into our ranks and marched away to our respective locations.

The roads of France and Flanders are not ideal for marching over with full packs. The pavé centre with its uneven cobbles, and in wet weather, the muddy borders of soft earth, do not make ideal courses. We now made our first acquaintance with these straight, tree-lined ways, evidently built by military engineers, with that one obsession at the back of Continental minds—War. Soon we heard the distant boom of guns and were thrilled, as any novice, with the sight of woolly bundles in the skies, the work of anti-aircraft gunners. Our way lay through the Foret de Nieppe, on through Merville to Estaires. Here the 133rd and the 134th were accommodated while the 132nd found a home at Morbecque. The 134th Field Ambulance spending the first night at Boesinghem.

The first march was to us crammed with interest, helping considerably to fortify our feet. The quaint little homesteads of Northern France, with the cross worked into the tiles of the gabled roofs. The large wheels attached to the sides of these little farmsteads, worked by a dog, treadmill fashion, for churning purposes within the kitchen. The wayside shrines of which we had heard so much, and ever and anon the signs of war denoted by captive balloons and passing aeroplanes. We noticed too, with interest, the general use of dogs in drawing rather large carts for their size, filled, too often, by the bulky owners. To say nothing of the unequal yoking of oxen and ponies in the creaking agricultural vehicles of these parts. At night we were to see the constant rise and fall of Verey lights illuminating

EASTBOURNE

THE BORGIAS

the darkness, hear the rat-tat-tat of machine gun fire, and the sharp report of sporadic artillery.

We now received that essential portion of our complement, the mechanical transport, in the shape of the Motor Ambulances, Fords and Sunbeams, which were added to our strength. The work which the former accomplished, made possible by their high clearance, was amazing. To say nothing of the intrepidity of their drivers. On the occasion of attacks the Fords were used almost into the Front Line.

Our arrival in France was at a time when the fighting was passing through a space of quiet. The area to which we were drafted, now comparatively still, was historic by reason of much bloodshed. Names had arisen of little places grown to momentous significance by reason of the heroisms of regiments and individuals. Two battles had been fought around the shambles that was Ypres. Lens and Neuve Chapelle had provided a bloody sacrifice of England's youth. Hill 60 had been won at the cost of hard fighting. Festubert, Givenchy and Loos had added lustre to British Arms, given numerous V.C's a local habitation and a name, and rendered many a home sad with the memory of those who would never return. But the Somme was not yet nor the bloody fighting of St. Julien and Passchendale.

Sir John French had been succeeded by Sir Douglas Haig, while many reputations, both at home and on the battle front, were in the balance. Fraternising had taken place between the opposing forces at the Second War Christmas just passed.

The observer as he entered the War zone could not but be impressed by the immense amount of organisation that had taken place during those eventful months. True the struggle had settled down to one of stagnation, relieved by raids and strafes, but the order which had been brought out of chaos spoke highly for the staff work which had been done. The foundation of all the future fighting had been well and truly laid. We entered a field, mapped out and prepared, benefiting greatly by the labour and sacrifice of others. The serried rows of Guardsmen's crosses in Poperinghe Cemetery, told, as they now tell, how England stood before the greatest onslaught of her time, in the Salient we were later to know so well.

A word should be said at this point concerning the formation of the 39th Division to which we belonged. It was composed of Kitchener troops (with the exception of one Brigade), commanded by Major-Gen. N. W. Barnardiston, M.V.O. Three battalions of the Sussex Regiment, the 11th, 12th and 13th, known as "Lowther's Lambs," who had seen training at Cooden Beach, Bexhill, with the 14th Hampshire Regiment, formed the 116th Infantry Brigade commanded by Brig.-Gen. J. E. Watson.

The 117th Brigade under Brig.-Gen. P. Holland,. C.B., was composed of the 17th King's Royal Rifle Corps; the 16th Rifle Brigade and the 16th and 17th Notts and Derby Regiment.

Then came a Territorial Brigade, under Brig.-Gen. W. Bromilow, comprising the 1/1st Herts., the 1/1st Cambs., and the 6th Cheshire and the 4/5th Royal Highlanders or Black Watch. This

Brigade, which came to be known as the 118th, had been out in France long since, seen much fighting and took their place as part of our Division upon our arrival in the Estaires district.

The 13th Gloucester Regiment was the pioneer battalion, whilst the Field Artillery was comprised of the 174th, 179th and 186th Brigades, R.F.A. The Royal Engineers consisted of the 225th, 227th and 234th Field Companies, R.E., whilst the Divisional Train, A.S.C., and ourselves, completed the Division.

The Medical Services were under the A.D.M.S., Colonel G. W. Brazier-Creagh, C.M.G., of whom more anon., with Major C. R. Millar as the D.A.D.M.S.

It should be mentioned that a Division contains three Field Ambulances each of which is comprised of 180 men, and is divided into a Bearer and Tent (or Nursing Division). The Ambulances are also divided into three Sections, A, B, C, which are capable of working independently of one another and are again divided into Bearer and Tent sub-divisions.

Our first work was of a light and initial nature, for we had still much to learn, and consisted chiefly in the running of Divisional Rest Stations and the care of sick, rather than wounded. One of these was at the Chateau Morbecque with its beautiful grounds which was taken over by the 132nd Field Ambulance. B-section of this unit also establishing small dressing stations at Steenbecque, La Belle Hostesse and Blaringhem.

Whilst the other was at the College, Estaires, which was occupied by the 133rd Field Ambulance. The 134th Field Ambulance took over a hospital at the Pensionnat des Demoiselles at Estaires.

The College would, of course, suggest to the unfledged ear, cool green lawns and cloistered walks, but disillusionment was complete when its barracky nature was discovered. The top floor, which had been used as a small theatre, served as a billet, whilst less fortunate ones found accommodation lower down the Doulieu Road in outhouses. Soon after arrival some eighty rats were killed in this latter hostel, their bodies being laid out in rows for the C.O's inspection. One man placed his mess tin on a beam overhead in this place and during the night an exploring rat knocked it down, scoring a direct hit on the unfortunate owner's head.

Although Morbecque was so attractive externally yet many became lousy here and remained so for duration.

Estaires was a somewhat dirty little town, with mud besmattered walls, complete with its Church, Square, Hotel de Ville, and not least, the Café du Commerce. Very characteristic of Northern France as we were to discover, yet it held the amenities of a few shops where blacking, soap and tooth powder vied with lace, post cards and eatables in one common display. Here we were introduced to the everlasting stand-by of hungry Tommies—eggs, chips and coffee. Cognac and the dear delights of over-crowded estaminets with the nightly game of House, provided variation for those who indulged their fancies in stronger things. Here, too, we met with admiration the old timers, men who had been out since 1914 and therefore knew all there was to know of the eternal war. Tunnellers with their thigh boots, on mysterious missions in the line, spent their hours here between their labours in the trenches.

Many of the houses in Estaires lay back from the road and a slimy ditch ran by their front gates. One or two men in search of kindly women to wash their clothes, having deposited their bundles, took a short cut out after leaving madame, with the result that in the darkness, missing the little bridged gateway, they fell headlong in the mire.

An institution of abiding memory, the Baths, was part of our work here, under the charge of Lieut. R. C. Cooke, situated in an old brewery. This consisted of vats of varying size and depth. The method of procedure was that one soaped and prepared one's dirty body in the shallow pool and finished off the rinsing stage by climbing a ladder into the larger vat. Heaven help the man who swallowed a mouthful of those deep and soapy waters !

Officers were bathed here and a tale is told of one, a colonel with monocle complete, appearing at closing time, asking for a " belly-bath—what ! " Arrangements were made, towels laid from the disrobing room to the aforesaid vats. The colonel duly walks across the way of towels and drops into the water. After a time, during which he swims round the bath, he is assisted out by the orderly. More towels are placed on the ground, and holding the orderly's hand, in his birthday suit, he is escorted back to the dressing room. Result, much satisfaction by a refreshed colonel and five francs for the orderly.

Whilst in the Estaires area detachments were sent to various Field Ambulances of another Division for instruction in the future work. Some to the 25th Field Ambulance, at Nouvieu Monde, others to the 26th Field Ambulance at Doulieu. and a party from the 134th Field Ambulance to Bac Ste Maur to a special abdominal ward. Here we were initiated into the art of nursing, painting Sergeant-Major's knees with iodine, administering Mist Expec. and number Nines, and became acquainted more fully with the Army pharmaco-pœia. We also became conversant with that small but important publication known as the Army Nomenclature of Diseases, outside of which no soldier could die. It contained a variety of complaints, chief of which were N.Y.D. and P.U.O., initials allowing of varying interpretations. As far as records show, however, no one of the officers was guilty of that banal diagnosis of G.O.K.

Others were conveyed after dark, into the line to the A.D.S. at Green Barn near Neuve Chapelle to learn the evacuation of wounded. One member of this party received a bullet wound in the cap, the signs of which he proudly exhibited on return, whilst one man of the 132nd Field Ambulance was shot through the thigh.

Just, however, as we were settling down to the life in and about Estaires, orders came for a move. The detachments were called in and our heavy feet once again made acquaintance with the pavé. Out from Estaires we marched across the little bridge over the Lys into La Gorgue, which adjoined Estaires and which was notorious for cock fights, usually held on a Sunday.

The 132nd Field Ambulance proceeded to Gonnehem on the 27th March and then to Robecque on the 31st where the Mill Dressing Station was taken over. While the 133rd Field Ambulance marched to Calonne-sur-la-Lys on March 26th, and the 134th Field Ambulance to Zelobes on the 27th. From here on April 3rd a section of the Ambulance was sent to Vielle Chapelle for instruction.

This march again provided great interest. Past the white-washed walls of quiet homesteads with lichened roofs that had echoed to the marching troops of Wellington's campaigns, now pock-marked by shell fire. Over canals with their quaint drawbridges. By the steam tramways that plied along the roadside about these parts, drawn by dirty, primitive and smoky engines with a shrill whistle.

At Calonne a scabies hospital was taken over and we were instructed in the use of sulphur baths, whilst the famous Thresher machine that burnt 2 cwt. coal in four hours and raised 10 lbs. pressure to the square inch disinfected the scabious wearing apparel. More baths were taken over at St. Venant, again under the charge of Lieut. R. C. Cooke.

Whilst in this district the spring rains, which seemed to continue for the rest of the year for that matter, were much in evidence. Rain was an almost continuous development, so that the Lys was full to overflowing, as also its tributaries.

The 8th Division, which consisted of several Bantam Battalions, was now on the march and we heard these poor devils trudging along those squelching slushy roads, throughout the night, in pouring rain, whilst we sought sleep in rat-infested barns. Yet, withal these marchers were cheerful and relieved the way with irrepressible songs. We also discovered the amenities of farm-house kitchens, sat round those curious little stoves, with their one red spot, drank milk and partook of innumerable eggs, and generally made ourselves agreeable to madame and mademoiselle. The latter to our astonishment was a curious mixture of the slattern and the mannequin. Who can forget her appearance at early morning, how she toileted in a basin no larger than one used for sugar and appeared in the afternoon in the daintiest of creations !

Now was the thrifty husbandman busy in his field. But as no great harvest can be obtained without fertilisation of the soil, so some will remember with olfactory sorrow, the spreading out upon the ground the contents of the local cesspools. This was usually pumped up by hand power into barrel-shaped carts, the daughter of the house supervising arrangements. No German chemist ever produced such smell with any gas he ever fulminated. Sunday was too often the day chosen on which to pollute the air, for miles around, with this foul and forceful manure.

This area, with its trim little fields, pollarded willows and neat farmsteads, became very attractive to us. There was an air of cleanliness about its greenness that was refreshing, whilst the War was sufficiently far away to trouble us but little.

Impromptu concerts were now in evidence, though these were not always in the best taste. Perhaps a healthier outlet for pent-up feelings was found in the football matches of which several were played here. One of these being rather memorable as the only three balls available were popped after 20 minutes play!

Trips to Merville relieved the monotony, with its fascinating collection of gabled roofs and its shops and canteens. Here we enjoyed ourselves according to our tastes and within the limitations of the last pay-day. The Church was worthy of mention, a modern structure replacing several earlier foundations, as its series of windows told. These beautiful stained glasses represented a sad and chequered history of pillaging, fire and destruction of the earlier Merville and its Church. Alas ! 1918 was to see again the town sacked and destroyed, its Church razed to the ground, when the Germans made their advance and both Estaires and Merville fell into their hands.

The severity and sanguinariness of the War was soon felt, as indicated by the following somewhat naive entry made by one of the O.C's in the War Diary. "The stationery boxes do not contain nearly enough forms for the working of a D.R.S. and F.A. combined. A typewriter and duplicator would be of great assistance."

To say nothing of the occasions when men on rest from the line, with all its mud and death, were paraded in as large numbers as possible, to hear read extracts on Military law. Usually ending with threats of dire punishment that might be theirs and the monotonous refrain about being shot at dawn.

Having now become acclimatised to the surroundings and the work, our Division proceeded to take its place in the line. We relieved the 38th Division in the Givenchy and Festubert Sectors of the XI Corps Front, the change being completed by the 20th April. We now become part of the First Army commanded by General Sir C. Munro, G.C.B.

The 116th Infantry Brigade moved up from Les Lauriers to the Locon area on the 14th and took over the trenches in the Givenchy Sector on the 15th. The 117th Brigade now commanded by Brig.-Gen. R. D. F. Oldman, D.S.O., moved up from La Gorgue and Merville to Vielle Chapelle on the 14th, occupying the trenches in the Festubert Sector on the 16th. Whilst the 118th Brigade moved from Gonnehem and Bethune area to the Locon district on the 16th and went into Divisional reserve.

In consequence of this the 132nd Field Ambulance took over a small chateau as a hospital from the 129th Field Ambulance at Bois de Pacaut on the 18th April, but on the 22nd, A and B-section of the unit moved back to Robecque leaving C-section to run the chateau as a hospital for the sick of the Division. During their stay here C-section enjoyed a very pleasant spirit that existed between officers and men. The good qualities of Lieut. S. A. Walker, later killed, were particularly evident. The Sergeants entertained the Officers to dinner here and a very merry evening was spent.

Noticing an absence of personnel one morning when they should have been in evidence, Lieut. Walker proceeded to the billet, flung open the door and yelled, " Hi, come along you fellows, are you waiting for the Resurrection? " There was a rustling of garments in consequence that had no relationship with cerements.

The 133rd Field Ambulance now moved to the White House at Essars, with its pleasant little gardens, on April 19th, taking over from the 129th Field Ambulance and on the 27th received a visit of inspection from the D.D.M.S., XI Corps, Colonel R. H. Firth.

The 134th Field Ambulance proceeded to Mesplaux Farm on the 18th April, when a D.R.S. was taken over. Mesplaux was an unusually large farm for this portion of France and consisted of a series of capacious buildings which enclosed the usual middens, the whole being surrounded by a wide moat. The stagnant water of the ponds and the moat gave considerable trouble to the sanitary instincts of the officer in charge. The place was alleged to date from 1716 and to have been used by Napoleon. Accommodation was available for 100 patients and 10 officers.

Whilst here, on May 16th, Lieut. J. H. Porter was promoted Captain and became second in command, and on the 18th the D.M.S. of the First Army, Surgeon-Gen. Pike, paid a visit of inspection, when he expressed pleasure at what he saw. This was followed on May 20th, by an inspection by the G.O.C. XI Corps, Lieut.-Gen. Sir R. C. Haking, K.C.B. On the 22nd, Lieut. Tutt left the unit having been posted as M.O. to the 1/1st Cambs. On May 30th, Major Honeybourne was evacuated sick; appendicitis had supervened and an operation was essential. His departure was an occasion of great and mutual regret. He had the men paraded in order to bid them farewell, when before he could say a word, an exceedingly un-military cheer broke out that was sufficient to show their feelings and relationship. He was succeeded as O.C. by Major H. C. Hildreth on June 2nd.

Some excitement was caused during the unit's occupancy of this farm by a fire which broke out in the cookhouse. Not, perhaps, an unusual occurrence in such a place. The occasion, however, was immortalised by the N.C.O. who reported to the O.C., " The fire was distinguished at 3 a.m.! " The Forward Posts for which we were now responsible were as follows: An A.D.S. at Marais and Aid Posts at Rue de Cailloux, Barnton Road and Festubert. These were controlled from Mesplaux Farm.

The M.D.S. at Essars was responsible for Lone Farm, Givenchy as an A.D.S. with Aid Posts at South More, Lambeth Road, Queens' Road and Sidbury. The route of evacuation was via Hitchin Road and Birdcage Walk to Southmore, thence to A.D.S., Queen's Road and Old Wolf's Road to Queen's Road Relay Post and Orchid Road and Gunner Walk to Sidbury.

Lone Farm was the shell of an old square building, situated between Westminster Bridge on the La Bassee Canal and Windy Corner, which was the entrance to the trenches. The courtyard was flanked on two sides by a high wall, but was open to the canal side. The dressing and receiving rooms were housed in the cellar, a long, tubular apartment, badly ventilated. At night cars came up as far as the courtyard, but were never allowed past Westminster Bridge during the day. A battery of 18-pounders lived in dug-outs between the A.D.S. and the canal, and relieved the monotony at night by their flashes and incessant bark.

Not far away was Windy Corner, so named without any reference to meterological conditions, and was the entrance to the trenches which were reached through a derelict baker's shop. At this period of the year these communication trenches were particularly beautiful, producing many spring wild flowers behind the wire netting that protected their crumbling sides. Nature had a peculiar and effective way of discounting men's destructive powers, which was particularly noticeable here. Bullets, both machine gun and rifle, used to whistle and expend themselves in the dust at night, between Windy Corner and the A.D.S.

Many, too, will remember the cemetery, then all too full, that lay on the left of the road going trench-wards, just past Lone Farm. And the strong-smelling weed that had overgrown these graves. The mortuary was just opposite, where the bodies awaited until they could be conveyed to a less crowded resting place. It is understood that in that little cemetery, now one of those beautiful English oases, was buried a friend of H.R.H. the Prince of Wales, who sometimes visits the spot now. An amusing and characteristic incident is told by one man whilst doing duty at Lone Farm.

He had gone into the trenches with an officer and was returning alone when he came across a very small Tommy who had been wounded in the foot. Realising the difficulties of getting a stretcher along he decided to carry his small comrade in his arms. Presently he encountered some more of the battalion coming up, so he put his foot on a ledge and propped the boy across his knee in order to give them room to pass. Instantly one of them shouted, " Hallo, Sparrer, has yer dad been spanking yer? " " Nah, " replied Sparrer, " but 'e ses muvver won't let me play soldiers no more! "

Life at this time and on this Front, was particularly pleasant. There was the excitement of being actually in the danger zone, with definite work to do, though not too much, and the unfamiliar scene of desolation and ruin. We bathed in the shell holes, basked in the sun and played football in the open courtyard. With this first acquaintance with the line souvenir hunting was indulged in by many, though it was soon discovered that nose caps and pieces of shrapnel gathered in sufficient quantities weighed rather heavily. While unexploded German shells becoming too numerous were left to lie by the roadside. It was discovered, too, that one could not wear more than three or four aluminium rings at one time with comfort. Another form of relaxation was quoit playing by means of old horse shoes made into rings by the farriers, A.S.C.

We now came in contact with that mass friendship which seemed to exist between the troops, and which found expression in the general use of " chum " as a means of address. Yet, too, there existed that curious psychological attitude of one man to another, which caused a man to covet portions of the kit of his wounded friend, because it was better than his own. Perhaps this was an attempt, in bowing to the inevitable, to seek what personal benefit another's misfortune could bestow. After all, one's belongings were few, life was reduced to the minimum, and in too short a time they might be at the disposal of the first comer.

The Officers' Mess at Essars was at this time enriched and enlivened by a French interpreter who was attached to the Ambulance. The following extract from a private diary is illuminating and requires no comment. " Monsieur is a most entertaining Frenchman. Typical, fiery, enthusiastic, continental. Most expressive eyes I have ever seen. Full of gestures and sentiment. Rides a horse fairly well. Has a room above the mess where I found him one morning attired in pink silk pyjamas, reclining on his bed, which was adorned with charming coloured rugs and cushions. Whole room pervaded with delicate scent. He is by way of being an artist in water colours."

Bethune, with all its waterways, was the Mecca of this district in which we now found ourselves. Who will forget its pleasant tree-lined roads, the shops that enclosed the cobbled square and the gabled, ancient roofs that gave an air of friendly mediævialness to the old town. The tower, with its belfry high over the quaint old shops that stood in the middle of the Square and its magnificent old Church. The War had troubled this pleasant place but little.

Needless to say Bethune provided a thousand joys to relieve the life of a soldier. All tastes were catered for from the house of ill-fame to the Gospel meetings held in rooms above the shops. Pleasant were the hours spent within its boundaries. The officers made use of the Au Paon d'Or or the Cafe du Globe, where champagne cocktails could be had for the asking; to say nothing of the Officers' Club. While the men enjoyed various restaurants, according to their means, and the entertainment companies that here gave good shows. There were many attractive shops, some made more attractive by the assistants who served within them, notably a boot shop in a side street where two engaging damsels conducted a flourishing business. The complex of the time, however, credited these two with being spies.

Sad is it to relate that the old Bethune of Hugo's days passed entirely away and a new town has since sprung up that resembles not the old.

Bethune Square was the scene of a very remarkable gathering on Sunday, August 6th, when a commemoration service was held to mark the beginning of the third year of the War. The Square was literally packed with troops and a memorable sermon was preached by the Chaplain-Gen. Bishop Taylor Smith, on a text taken from the Book of Joshua, " All that thou commandest us we will do, and whithersoever thou sendest us, we will go." It was a magnificent sight to see the whole Square become a mass of glittering bayonets as the troops ported arms and gave the salute as one man, ere they marched away.

MESPLAUX FARM

LONE FARM, GIVENCHY

All was quiet on the Western Front for some weeks after we made our entrance into the line. Relief followed relief, with an occasional raid, until the night of the 16/17th June when the 35th Division was withdrawn and the Corps Front was now held by only three Divisions. The 39th was the centre Division, with the 33rd on the right and the 61st on the left. Our Division was now responsible for the Ferme du Bois and the Festubert Sub-sections, the front extending from Grenadier Road to Oxford Street.

In consequence of this the 132nd Field Ambulance moved to Vielle Chapelle on the 17th June and took over from the 105th Field Ambulance the A.D.S. at St. Vaast, and Plum Street and Factory Posts. While C-section of the unit took over the skin hospital at Calonne. It should be noted, too, that Daylight Saving came into force on June 14th, for the first time.

On June 19th the 133rd Field Ambulance moved its Headquarters to Zelobes where a M.D.S. was taken over from the 106th Field Ambulance. The A.D.S. at Lone Farm, Givenchy, with its various posts was handed over to the 33rd Division, while the A.D.S. at Rue du Bois was in turn taken over with its Posts at Path House, Tube Station and King George's Relay Post. Work was now carried out in the latter post by the unit. A holding party consisting of one section had been left at the White House, Essars.

The A.D.S. at Rue du Bois was in the Tuning Fork Road, between Le Touret and Rue L'Epinette, just behind Festubert Village, and consisted of a huge sand-bagged barn behind an estaminet. The dressing and receiving rooms were housed in elephants heavily sand-bagged. Incidentally, the estaminet was still inhabited by an old couple and their daughter, the father and mother being held in great suspicion as spies. The old man used to drive his cattle into unlikely pastures up the La Bassee Road, and when later he took to white-washing, two detectives were sent up to watch his activities. Quite a number of other civilians lived here, including little Suzanne with her mother and father, with whom the O.C. A.D.S. was billeted. On one occasion when shelling took place Suzanne was almost hit by the first shell over. From here also some small baths were run at Grub Street. The line at Festubert consisted of a series of outposts or islands, which had little or no connection with one another, and were manned by one or two men apiece. The trenches could hardly be described as " dug " here, the ground being so boggy, but were built of sandbags above the level of the ground. It was from these " islands " that the Division received so many casualties.

On the 30th June the first attack of any considerable size in which the Division had been engaged was carried out at Richebourg St. Vaast, directed against the Boar's Head. The assaulting battalions were those of the 11th and 12th Royal Sussex Regiment. This abortive raid—for such in reality it was—proved to be a costly and bloody combat as far as the two battalions were concerned, and was but little commented upon in official reports. It was evidently designed to draw attention from the activities on the Somme which were then maturing.

The medical arrangements were in the hands of the 132nd Field Ambulance, Lieut. D. J. MacDougall was in charge at the A.D.S., St. Vaast, which was a series of dug-outs situated in an orchard, there being no house or building to act as a shelter. Tram lines ran right into the place and were extremely useful. Lieut. G. T. Gimlette was in charge at Plum Street and Lieut. J. B. Dunning at Factory Post. Assistance was also provided with bearers from the 133rd Field Ambulance. Some 655 cases, consisting of 21 officers and 634 O.R's were passed through the M.D.S. within 24 hours.

This being the first serious work in which the medical units were employed some minor mistakes were made. These were pointed out in a very kind manner by the D.D.M.S. for our future guidance and improvement. For instance, too much attention was paid to dressing cases at the A.D.S., resulting in too slow an evacuation and a consequent danger of congestion. On this occasion Lieut. E. F. Nivin was slightly wounded, but remained at duty, and 10 O.R's of the 132nd Field Ambulance were wounded. Another of the wounded, Private W. Daniels showed considerable pluck and devotion to duty. Although wounded he refused to be evacuated from the dug-out until the others had been removed, and assisted in placing the cases on stretchers, working on his hands and knees.

Later when the 132nd Field Ambulance was at Mesplaux news was received that the Corps Commander, under authority from the Commander-in-Chief, had

bestowed the M.M. on the following for gallantry
and devotion to duty:—
    65863   S/Sergeant F. A. Hodges.
    65868   Private W. Daniels.
    65884   Lance Corporal E. T. Fairbrother.

Two other raids were carried out. One on the
night of the 3/4th July by the 16th Rifle Brigade
and the 17th Notts and Derby Regiments, directed
against the Pope's Nose. On this occasion the
134th Field Ambulance was in action for the first
time. The casualties numbered 87, many of them
being seriously wounded. Evacuation was carried
out over the open along Barnton Road, past the
R.A.P., and from thence to the A.D.S., Marais;
also along Quinque Rue to Festubert Relay Post
and from thence to the A.D.S.

The following were mentioned as having done
particularly good work on this occasion:—
    Major H. C. Hildreth.
    Captain J. H. Porter.
    Lieutenant H. Mitchell.
    Lieutenant G. W. Racey.
    Lieutenant G. W. Huggins.
    72207   S/Sergeant J. Gardner.

The second raid was carried out by the 17th King's
Royal Rifle Corps and the 16th Notts and Derby
Regiments on the night of the 11/12th July. On
this occasion the 133rd and the 134th shared the
responsibilities of the work of evacuation. Casualties
numbering 81 passed through their hands and all
the work was carried out in a highly satisfactory
manner. The evacuation was as follows. For the
17th King's Royal Rifle Corps via Quinque Rue to

R.A.P., thence to Festubert Collecting Post and on to Marais and the M.D.S. at Bethune. For the 16th Notts and Derby Regiment via Rope Trench to R.A.P., thence to A.D.S. at Rue du Bois. Two dressing stations had been established at Marais, one for walking and one for lying cases.

Captain W. P. H. Munden, M.O. in charge 16th Notts and Derby's and the following men of the 133rd Field Ambulance were particularly mentioned as having done conspicuous work:—

    72147   Private L. Finch.
    78203   Private H. Meighan.
    72133   Private J. W. Jolly.
    72011   Private W. A. Willis.

The next day three men of the 133rd Field Ambulance were wounded, and buried in a trench by shell fire whilst carrying a patient. They were Corporal Dean, Privates Beard and Whiteley. They first extricated themselves and then their patient and although themselves wounded took him to the A.D.S. Private Cavadesca, seeing their plight, went to their assistance although he was taking another wounded man to the A.D.S. A letter of congratulation was later sent to all four of the party.

A raid was also carried out by the Cambs., Cheshire and Herts. Regiments combined on July 19th, followed by another made by the Cambs. on the 22nd. For that matter, the Division seemed to specialise in raids, many of them being made by our men with blackened faces. The casualties presented a somewhat minstrel-like appearance when brought in.

On July 6th the 132nd Field Ambulance moved into Bethune taking over a M.D.S. at the Civil and Military Hospital. It also took over an A.D.S. at Harley Street, though still retaining the A.D.S. at St. Vaast. In like manner the 133rd Field Ambulance took over the Ecole Maternelle at Bethune on the 7th, having handed over Zelobes to the 2/3rd Field Ambulance of the 61st Division and proceeded to take over an A.D.S. at Cambrin, still retaining the A.D.S. at Rue du Bois under Captain B. M. Hunter. Baths were also taken over at Grubb Street and Gorre, while two men still retained the bath at Essars.

The 134th Field Ambulance moved to Annezin on the 7th and took over a D.R.S. from the 101st Field Ambulance. The A.D.S., Lone Farm, was also taken over by Captain J. H. Porter and Lieut. R. I. Harris, whilst Lieut. Simpson was sent to Marais. The Divisional Laundry and Baths at Bethune and Baths at Annequin were put under the charge of this Ambulance. During the tenure of Givenchy, Private Lack of the unit was wounded.

Whilst at Lone Farm a swarm of bees was hived in an improvised and specially-built box by Lieut. Harris, assisted by one other rank attired in his gas mask. This proved a great attraction until some ruthless hand swept the whole away and Materlinck Republic was no more.

During July Lieut. S. J. L. Lindeman left the 133rd Field Ambulance, having been posted to medical charge of the 16th Notts and Derby Regiment.

The A.D.S. at Cambrin was in a cottage under the walls of the ruined Church, which had probably been the Cure's house. The Receiving and Dressing rooms were in the sand-bagged cottage itself, whilst the personnel were housed in dug-outs in the garden. The cellar of the cottage, which was large, had been rigged up to accommodate stretcher cases in the event of shelling. The entrance, however, was difficult of access and almost impossible for badly wounded cases. Several Aid Posts in the trenches were served from here and a considerable number of men were required to staff these. Lieut. R. C. Cooke and Lieut. J. W. Wayte were in charge.

The Church had been badly smashed and across one jagged hole hung an untouched Crucifix, one of those peculiar phenomena of the War. Another feature of interest was an unexploded shell that had torn a way through the wall and lodged in the one opposite. The nose visible outside, the base inside the ruined building. The Church was used as a mortuary, the dead remaining here until the Padre could come and bury them in the Churchyard, a portion of which, that was all too full, having been set aside as a military cemetery. A large brick building adjacent was used as a canteen and soup kitchen. These were supervised by the Ambulance running the A.D.S. A communication trench commenced between the cottage and the canteen building, while a trolley line ran parallel with this as far as an artillery O.P. known as Maison Rouge. A railway line towards Vermelles was found useful for evacuating wounded in trucks, being brought by this means into Cambrin.

Opposite the A.D.S. was a little shop where an old woman still lived who sold candles and chocolate.

Such was the tenacity and temerity of these villagers to their home and surroundings.

Incidentally the A.D.S. was found to be in a filthy state when taken over and much time had to be spent in cleaning up and putting in order. Hunting rats, sand-bagging and white-washing were the pastimes indulged in here.

The 39th Division took over the Corps Front from La Bassee Canal to Oxford Street on the 16th July and in consequence the 132nd Field Ambulance moved to Mesplaux Farm on the 15th. On the 23rd this unit handed over the A.D.S. at St. Vaast to the 31st Division and took over the A.D.S. at Rue du Bois from the 133rd Field Ambulance carrying on the evacuation from the front line through the R.A.P's at Path House and Rue de Cailloux. The 133rd Field Ambulance in turn handed over the A.D.S. at Cambrin to the 24th Field Ambulance and the personnel returned to the Headquarters at Bethune. Later, on the 24th, the Ambulance again took over Essars and Lone Farm, Givenchy. On the 1st August the hospital at Bethune was inspected by the G.O.C. of the Division who expressed himself as pleased with what he saw.

Whilst in possession of the A.D.S. at Lone Farm on this occasion, an extremely sad incident occurred. Two prisoners were brought up over night, housed in a special apartment rigged up by the Engineers in the cellar of the A.D.S. and shot the next morning, outside the flanking walls. The personnel under pain of heavy penalties had been ordered to keep inside their quarters, but could not but hear the words of command, the tread of marching feet and the final shots. The impression left was a lasting one. Our own men placed crosses over those newly-dug graves.

August 7th was memorable as being the day when the enemy shelled Bethune. The 33 C.C.S. was badly damaged and some of the nurses were wounded. The civilian population was thrown into a panic and many casualties were sustained by them. The 133rd Field Ambulance organised stretcher squads to assist in clearing the wounded from the streets, and whilst doing so in the Belfry Square sustained their first casualty in Private P. A. Brown, who was severely wounded and later died. His funeral was attended by a party of his comrades.

The 134th Field Ambulance at Annezin acted as the Clearing Ambulance for these casualties, dealing with some 200 cases. The total casualties during the bombardment amounted to approximately 1,500. Whilst in this district two changes took place in the Divisional Command. Major-Gen. R. Dawson, C.B., assumed command vice Major-Gen. N. Barnardiston on June 10th. Whilst General Dawson was in turn succeeded by Major-Gen. G. J. Cuthbert, C.B., C.M.G., on July 13th.

The A.D.M.S. of the Division was also responsible for certain sanitary arrangements, as distinguished from the medical units. These included in the area a Laundry and Bath at Locon, Bath at Le Touret, which emitted much smoke and drew enemy fire, and baths at Gorre, Le Quesnoy and Essars. These were, of course, staffed from the various Field Ambulances.

It should also be mentioned that the 82nd Sanitary Section, under the command of Captain C. H. Lilley, formed part of the medical units of the Division under the A.D.M.S. The work of this small body was entirely devoted to the sanitary side of Army life, the men being specially recruited for the purpose. The unit was a territorial establishment with H.Q. at Chelsea. Later they became Corps troops and ceased to move with us from place to place.

Although our task was mainly concerned with the sick and wounded of the Regiments which we served, yet we had to make ourselves generally useful to the civilian population with whom we came in contact. Hence on one occasion an officer and a sergeant were called upon to attend a confinement. It would be of great interest to hear the sergeant's version of the unusual rôle of mid-wife which he played that night. On another occasion a woman was taken into the A.D.S. at Lone Farm. She had unfortunately been wounded by a " dud " anti-aircraft shell, which, in falling had taken off one of her breasts and the top of the fingers of one hand. This, whilst she was holding a baby in her arms, the baby being unscathed. Then there were civilians' teeth to be extracted and minor ailments to be attended to; though it is not recorded that dental patients returned for a second dose at the hands of impromptu surgeons.

There were also innumerable other jobs found for us to fill up any spare time that might occur in the day's routine. We made horse lines and bits of roads, sprayed stagnant ponds with formaldehyde

and endeavoured to sanitise the middens around
which the farms were built. In some cases this was
done much against the owner's inclinations. We
also made an intimate acquaintance with the
brakish drinking water of these parts and never
succeeded in getting the taste of its chlorination
out of our mouths. The hard and impermeable
sub-stratum of soil was the cause of this metallic
water which was full of hidden peril for us, though
the native, by reason of his nativity, was immune.

It was whilst in this area that a private of one of
the Ambulances was tried by a F.G.C.M. for the
attempted use of a code in private letters to England.
The spy complex was in great evidence and here
was matter for a first class scandal. Some little
excitement, too, was caused when one of the horses
of the A.S.C. attached to the 133rd Field Ambulance
proved too frisky for Sergt. A. E. Bradley, A.S.C.,
of that unit, and backed into the ditch, breaking
the Sergeant's leg in so doing.

Our time, however, in these parts drew to its
inevitable close and our Division was relieved on
this Front on the nights of the 10/11th and 11/12th
August by the 30th and 31st Divisions, and we
were withdrawn into Army Reserve to the area
Auchel, Lozinghen, Allouane. We were destined
for the Somme where fighting of a considerable
nature had been waging for some weeks.

The journey on this occasion was made by route
march, taking some days to accomplish. The weather
was at its pleasantest and the countryside fast
ripening towards harvest. The dusty, tree-lined
roads wound in and out amid pleasant scenery,

varying as we travelled. We passed through the coal-producing district of Bruay with its pyramidal heap peculiar to that industry looking picturesque and Egypt-like against the setting sun. The marches were usually commenced in the late afternoon and carried on until the early hours of the next morning. Many wet shirts resulted ere we settled down in the clean straw of the barns provided for our rest and hospitality.

Numerous little incidents occurred to relieve the monotony of the journey, as for instance that provided by A-section of the 132nd Field Ambulance. These men were billeted for the night in a loft of a barn above some cows that occupied the ground floor. The men had gathered at the upper doorway and were encouraging the cooks to hurry up with the tea. To which the cooks were responding in the best cook-house strain, when suddenly the floor of the loft gave way, precipitating the thirsty marchers amid the cows. The laugh seemed to remain with the cooks !

We will follow the Ambulances in the order of their progress. The 132nd Field Ambulance having handed over Mesplaux to the incoming Division marched out on August 10th and crossing La Clarence River at Chocques proceeded to the small village of Allouagne. From here, the next day, they marched on to Magnicourt en Comte which they reached at 2 a.m. Nine a.m. that morning saw them again on the march which ended at Tincquettes, from which place an advance party was sent to the final area of destination at Acheux.

The 133rd Field Ambulance handed over Bethune to the 96th Field Ambulance on August 11th and proceeded to Auchel. From here they marched to Bailleul aux Corneilles on the 12th, where they stayed for about two weeks.

In like manner the 134th Field Ambulance vacated Annezin and marched to Rainbert on the 10th, reaching L'Abbaye Neuville on the 11th, where they bivouaced in the open, specialising in various types of domestic architecture. At this time mention was first made of an Ambulance Band, and whether it played the troops into step or out is not definitely known.

In the vicinity of St. Pol we were now concentrated for two weeks in quarters which were delightful indeed. A welcome contrast, in its summer splendour, against the flat fields of the Flanders we had just left. We, with our Division, now engaged in intensive training to fit us for the strenuous days that lay ahead. Route marches, drills, inspections and instructions were the orders of the day, while swimming and cricket filled up the intervals. This Arcadian existence suited us well.

THE A.D.M.S.

IT will hardly be out of place at this juncture to introduce to our readers a personality who moved amongst us during the time of our sojourn abroad. I refer to the A.D.M.S. of the 39th Division, Colonel George Washington Brazier-Creagh C.B., C.M.G. To belong to the medical services of the Division and not know the Colonel was a physical impossibility, for he seemed to be everywhere on all and every occasion. However, lest your memory has dimmed, let me describe him to you.

A man six feet in his socks, already greying with age, for his soldiering days were done before ours had commenced. But straight withal and muscular as one would expect of a regular. Bushy eyebrows, a moustache, a slightly cadaverous face and very white teeth. A brass hat that would persist in an angular attachment to the head, and a habit of punctuating his remarks with an emphatic sideways nodding of the same head. A pair of thin legs, denoting the horseman, for he had hunted with a pack of hounds in India, and a vocabulary that even a guardsman might envy. While on the left breast of his tunic were those little coloured strips that spoke of other wars than this and a wandering about Mother Earth to include India, China, Persia, South Africa and the Islands of the Sea. One would conclude, and rightly so too, that he knew his way about.

Of a soldiering family, with its seat at Creagh
Castle, County Cork, Colonel Brazier-Creagh came
down to us in a direct line from the Irish kings.
as the ancient history of that country shows.
Therefore one felt assured in his case of the truth
of the aphorism, an officer and a gentleman. Well
known as a gentleman rider in his younger days,
and hailed by all old regulars as one of them, he
exercised an individuality which only Ireland can
produce. Who could forget his demeanour or the
posteen coat that duly appeared in cold weather.

He had been employed by the Indian Government
on a Mission to Seistan and Baluchistan, and another
to China. Whilst in the South African War he
was O.C. for six months of one of the best-known
Ambulance Trains that ever plied on its mission of
succour in that campaign. Of this Sir Frederick
Treves in his Tale of a Field Hospital writes:
" Major Brazier-Creagh took as much pride in his
travelling hospital as if he had built it himself."
Lieut. Roberts was a patient in the train after being
wounded at Colenso. Later he served as S.M.O.
to the Imperial Light Horse and Lord Rawlinson's
Brigade. He had been retired some two years
before the Great War commenced, and had volunteered for service immediately on the outbreak of
hostilities. For some time prior to the inception
of our Division he was employed on various duties
overseas and returned from France to become
A.D.M.S., 39th Division.

The epitome of all his character, however, is
contained in his handwriting. A full and frank
confession of thick underlinings and slashes, with

splutterings and dots, expressing the idiosyncrasies that must out.

This, then, was the man selected to take charge of the medical services of the 39th Division. He commenced with the inception and remained to the very end of this hard-worked and finally shattered Division. A jealous guardian of the honour of the officers and men under his command and a persistent seeker after honours to be bestowed on those he felt proud to lead.

Generally speaking, his demeanour was austere and his sudden and numerous appearances were dis-comforting to both officers and men. He could strafe as few, and many can recall the personal lectures he bestowed on delinquients. Words fail to describe the occasion when he found two diphtheria suspects had been loaded in an ambulance with an officer pneumonia case! Yet no one was more appreciative of good and zealous conduct.

Not far beneath that faded tunic was a very warm heart belonging to this member of the Army List. How might it be reached? Quite effectively by the short and certain route of a good " hoss," that he could ride and judge, any old mongrel of a dog, or by a pet bird. In his contact with these was declared the man apart from the soldier; and they responded one and all, hailing him as their friend. A love of animals surely connotes a regard for one's fellow men !

If the Colonel could swear he could also pray, and did so night and morning. His Bible, too, well marked and thumbed, was always beside his bed, and was as well known to him as King's Regulations and the Racing Calendar. He could quote from the Book with some effect as he was known to do on one celebrated occasion when examining T.U. men in France.

"Do you read your bloody Bible?" asked he of one poor wight.

"No sir," replied the candid unfit.

"I thought not," continued the Colonel, "you read those cheap political newspapers! Well, it says in the Book, 'Whatsoever thy hand findeth to do, do it with all thy might.' Mark him light duty, Sergeant!" remarks he, aside, as he passes on.

That he had a decided bias towards those who hailed from the Green Isle was soon discovered, and was somewhat marked on another occasion at a T.U. parade, when one member disclosed that he came from Cork. "Oh!" says the Colonel, "d'you know the Hole in the Wall?"

"Yes," replies his crafty countryman.

"Well, you can get more than Mother's milk there, eh?" And the T.U's position was assured.

One of the Colonel's most characteristic possessions was the posteen coat already mentioned. This he was wont to assume on cold days with a somewhat tremendous result. He was known as the Mandarin in consequence. Witness then, the august spectacle of a visit from him thus attired, when the Ambulance was doing duty in the line. The traffic control stands aghast as he passes by in the Ford car seated by the driver, and he fails to salute. "Don't you salute when you see an officer?" asks the Colonel.

"Yes, sir," replies the aberrant one.

"Then why didn't you salute me?" No answer.

"What size boots dy'er wear?" asks the Mandarin of the astonished control, as he nudges the driver to proceed. And the driver thought he heard a chuckle.

Another possession, but this of a different category, was Jack, a mutilated magpie, with only one complete wing, who like Elias' Child Angel was wont to go with a lame gait all his days. How he used to screech his pleasure when the Colonel came near him. Perhaps it was the piece of raw meat he thought he detected, or perchance the affinity of a kind heart. The Colonel's ink, too, was good, as Jack well knew, for he drank of both red and black with the grace of a connoisseur. Afterwards it was reared all over the place with distressing results. Alas, poor Jack met an untimely end at the hands of an unsympathetic French woman. But she wished she hadn't when the Colonel reduced her to tears in the subsequent interview.

And one or two Frenchmen were glad to see the back of "l'Officier," when he wanted to know why their dogs were kept chained up day after day and thus reduced to a state of wretchedness and despair.

An old campaigner, the Colonel was not without experience in softening the hardships of active service, witness his own mess at headquarters, and his rather voluminous baggage, that was somewhat conspicuous at the numerous removals. But we can vouch on absolute authority that it contained no piano!

Abstemious, as all soldiers should be, the whiskey bottle lasted him a long time. But the menu of his table was as good as rail-head would allow, and there was usually a drum of choice cigars that sufficed to compensate for any failure in the commissariat. While after, or during the cigars, there was the " Spectator."

One sad case that called forth his pity and unavailing efforts to save, was the lad, an inmate of one of the Field Ambulances, who had deserted twice. He left no stone unturned to placate those in authority who took another view of the matter. There were, too, sundry conversations with Ambulance Commanders concerning the delinquiencies of certain junior officers who, may be, had supped too well. And certain references to having been young once, in an endeavour to soften the offence.

Needless to say the Colonel had one or two narrow squeaks, as did most who set their feet line-wards. But perhaps the narrowest was when he nearly got cut in two by one of those dirty little trains which ran by the Cloisters at Poperinghe. The car, the driver and himself escaped as by a hair's-breadth!

Another incident and we must conclude. Scene Locon or district.

" Has this man been evacuated? " asks the A.D.M.S.

" Yes, sir," replies the clerk.

" Then ther'll be bloody hell! "

That Colonel Brazier-Creagh was not perfect we will hardly dispute. A personality rich in character would suggest a collection of awkward opposites. One must judge by the sum total, and the perfect man was not found in any one of the Ambulances.

And now as,

"The Field
Strewn with its dank yellow drifts
Of withered leaves, and the elms,
Fade into dimness apace,
Silent . . . ."

we think kindly of this good warrior, and recall with pleasure the fulfilment of that little legend: *In Arduis Fidelis.*"

THE SOMME

THE scenery of the Somme was a pleasant contrast to that we had become accustomed to in the Bethune and Locon area. The rolling downs, reminiscent of Sussex, and the white roads threading here and there, gave cheerful encouragement to our imagination. Whilst the countryside, in the height of its summer glory, led us to believe we had entered upon a pleasant rustication. Around St. Pol the villages were ideally pretty, and flowers bedecked the gardens and the fields. The water, too, was drawn from deeper wells and was considerably better than that delivered from the pumps in and about Estaires. As, however, we drew nearer the line we found conditions more squalid, and such a plague of flies, as was never encountered since the days of Egypt. The sanitary conditions here had been sadly neglected.

Having enjoyed the training in the Third Army area and the conditions for some two weeks, we again went on trek. This time the 132nd Field Ambulance moved to Honval on the 23rd August, to Sus St. Leger on the 24th, to Bois du Warnimont on the 25th; and to the final scene of action at Acheux on the 27th. This Ambulance proceeded to erect a Divisional Collecting Station at Engle-belmer, with an A.D.S. at Mesnil.

The 133rd Field Ambulance left Bailleul aux Corneilles on the 23rd for Mesnil St. Pol; reaching Le Maraissec on the 24th; Authie on the 25th; and Vauchelles, their destination, on the 26th. Here a Field Ambulance site and a D.R.S. were taken over. The charger that carried Capt. Hunter and his 16 stone died en route. Toward the latter part of the journey the progress was slow owing to the congested state of the roads caused by the movement of troops.

Not to be outdone, the 134th Field Ambulance vacated L'Abbaye Neuville on the 22nd, making for Maiziers. From here they proceeded to Lucheaux on the 24th, reaching Bus les Artois on the 25th. From here B-section of this unit went to the A.D.S. at Mesnil, while the remainder took over a Corps Collecting Station from the 18th Field Ambulance at Acheaux, which consisted of a large number of marquees near the railway. The wounded could thus be evacuated by means of ambulance trains direct to the Base.

We were now in close proximity to Albert with its ruined streets, shattered houses, dismantled shops and derelict business premises. The chief feature of attraction was the comparatively modern basilica with its battered walls and the huge Madonna and Child leaning at right angles to the tower. Already the erstwhile emigres were drifting back, reopening the little shops and seeking to do what trade could be done amongst the floating population.

Our Division moved into the Beaumont Hamel Sector of the V Corps Front, Lieut.-Gen. A. E.

Fanshawe, C.B., Fifth Army under General Sir H. de la Poer Gough, K.C.B., on the evening of September 2nd. The 116th Infantry Brigade was on the right, the 117th Infantry Brigade on the left and the 118th Infantry Brigade in reserve.

The battle, or series of battles of the Somme, had, of course been waging since July 1st, and the heroism and dash of our troops, against tremendous odds, had filled England with both joy and sorrow. The mysterious and then unknown Tanks, had been used for the first time; one of the few surprises we were ever able to launch upon the Germans. It was, therefore, to no bed of roses that our Division was being called.

Preparations were at once pushed forward for an intended attack by the Division, and to meet requirements and the urgency of the situation a new A.D.S. known as Cookers was erected by the 134th Field Ambulance in a very short space of time, owing to the ingenuity and energy of Lieut. R. I. Harris, and consisted of a series of dug-outs made in the railway embankment facing the hill. On the other side of the embankment lay the Valley of the Ancre and beyond this the remains of Thiepval Woods and Thiepval Village. The hillside was covered with trenches, winding in and out, a chalky series of lines, English and enemy. The A.D.S. comprised a high and spacious bomb-proof dressing station, with a sand-bag guarded entrance and exit, fitted up with all the necessaries of an operating room. Part of the surroundings was paved with available bricks and duckboards were laid down. Two dumps were also established for the supply of dressings. One at Knightsbridge and the other at Hamel. R.A.P's were also established in the trenches. Right Sector, 4/5th Black Watch operating on right flank up the Valley of the Ancre, with two R.A.P's in Roberts Trench, another in Pottage Trench. Left Sector, R.A.P. in old German Trench and another R.A.P. in Knightsbridge. The Left Sector was manned with an advanced post at Knightsbridge and the A.D.S. at Mesnil, while the Right Sector advanced post was at Hamel with the A.D.S. at Cookers.

These posts were manned by the various Bearer Sub-Divisions of the Ambulances on the night of the 2nd September, in readiness for the attack on Beaumont Hamel on the morning of the 3rd, which at Zero hour was duly launched. That conditions were such as we had not encountered before is best expressed in the report of the A.D.M.S. on this occasion.

" The position occupied by our troops was one from which it was most difficult to evacuate owing to the ground being exposed and the line of evacuation a lengthy one. The entrenchments were dominated on three sides, the Aid Posts small and inadequate and exposed to shell and machine-gun fire. Added to this I am informed by officers commanding bearers and others that enemy snipers were most active, picking off our bearers when collecting, and wounding again the patients being carried on stretchers. Super-added to which were weather conditions which turned the frontal surroundings, roads and pathways into a boggy state.

A.D.S., Marais

Bringing in a Case by Wheeled Stretcher
Lone Farm

COOKERS, A.D.S.

THE CABSTAND, SOMME

Our casualties were heavy, amounting in all to 87, composed of 7 O.R's killed, 5 officers and 76 O.R's wounded. The killed were:—

Private Brunger.
Private Barton.
Private Crompton.
Private Steadman.
Private Mitchell.
Private Lewis.
S/Sgt. Gardner.

The officers wounded were :—

Lieut. W. S. T. Connel, M.O. in charge, 11th Royal Sussex.
Lieut. S. J. Darke, M.O. in charge, 16th Rifle Brigade.
Lieut. J. B. Dunning, M.O. in charge, 13th Royal Sussex.
Lieut. C. E. Tucker, O.C. Bearers, 132nd Field Ambulance.
Lieut. H. Mitchell, O.C. Bearers, 134th Field Ambulance.

The total casualties passing through the A.D.S. Divisional Collecting Station and M.D.S. up to 6 a.m. on September 5th were 41 officers and 1,336 other ranks. A feature of this and all subsequent attacks whilst on the Somme was the large number of wounded Germans that we were called upon to handle.

Some poignant scenes were witnessed on this occasion and acts of heroism performed which should be recorded in gold.

A description from one of the forward bearer-officers, Lieut. R. I. Harris, will convey something of the scene.

"Last night at 10.30 p.m., I took my party of 41 up to the battle Aid Post under the hill behind Roberts Trench. Tedious journey, stumbling along trenches filled with reserve troops. As many as could got in the dug-out, others made themselves shelters in the trench. In the dug-out were Wayte and his bearers, the padre Crawley, Dunning of the 13th Sussex, Cooke and myself.

The preliminary bombardment commenced at 5 a.m., exactly as grey dawn was breaking. Every gun firing at the same instant resulting in a deafening noise. Long crawling lines of infantry pushed through our bearers on their way to the jumping off point 50 yards ahead. In five minutes they charged. We could just see them outlined on the ridge across the river. A scattered mass of figures, running with wildly waving arms and legs, almost grotesque. From that time on the whole affair was one confused jumble of shells, noise, blood, wounded, stench, with only a few landmarks to mark off the time from any other time.

Contrary to expectation the wounded began to come in almost instantly after the commencement of the attack. By 5.30 a.m. the dug-out was jammed with patients and bearers. I started out with three picked bearers and a case at 6 a.m., cutting the obstructing wire in the Valley and along the road as I went. By this time the German barrage had developed into something worth while, but still the hill gave considerable shelter. From then on the bearers took down a constant stream of wounded. They were heroes—every bearer. They never hesitated to carry out my orders even when as the morning wore on the route became much more dangerous so that it was only a matter of time until every man who went down the road got hit. They carried on with a dogged persistence and an absolute indifference to personal danger. The wounded continued to pour into the Battle Aid Post so that all hands were full and a constant stream was sent on to Lieut. Mitchell in Hamel. Along the foot of the hill were the 13th Royal Sussex in support of the 11th Royal Sussex who had gone over. Each man had dug himself a little shelter into the hill. As the morning went on the Germans began to put their shells closer and closer to the foot of the hill. The back bursts caught the men in their shelters. Pretty soon instead of a line of living men they became a line of dead and wounded. It was gruesome to go along the foot of that hill, stumbling over men's legs and dead bodies of this and some earlier attack. The latter scattered about in contorted attitudes, their skins dark and dry like a mummy's.

Our men began to suffer heavy casualties. Every party almost who went down suffered some casualty. Lieut. Dunning was wounded in the back while dressing cases outside the dug-out. S/Sergt., 133, was wounded badly, and S/Sergt. Saunders severely. It was not until these went and several more bearers were either killed or wounded that I began to feel the gruesomeness of the situation. I felt broken up.

By 10 a.m. we began to realise that something was wrong as there was an ominous lull. Later it was discovered that we were back in our old trenches and the Germans back in theirs. The enemy barrage was terrible and presently a German sniper began to command the road and picked off anything that moved. He was responsible for some of our men and the patients and succeeded in closing the road to us.

During the intervening hours, and as soon as the bombardment ceased, we began to search the front line trenches for cases, and the Aid Post was soon full again. It was not until dark that these could be sent down.

At dusk I went down to Cookers and brought up 50 men of the Cambs. and one officer. These were soon loaded up with cases and sent down via Peche Street Trench. Difficulty was encountered at the first bend, but with two hours' digging this was overcome and the stream of wounded was sent down the straight portion. All night the cases crowded in and only by working with the utmost fury were they successfully cleared by daylight. The first portion of Peche Street was almost unsurmountable.

We reached Hamel at 6.30 a.m., a filthy, muddy lot, covered with blood and tired beyond description. From here the cases were sent by wheeled stretcher to Cookers."

One man writes that the bombardment was so severe that the earth trembled and cotton wool had to be placed in the ears to deaden the sound.

His description, too, of the bearers coming down the shell-swept road is vivid in the extreme.

"On bringing my second case down the road I looked behind and found two men coming with their case. All at once a great big shell burst. My pal and I let our stretcher down and we ducked. I looked round for those other lads and could not see them on account of the smoke. At last to our joy we found them coming along with their case too. We all got back to our relay post safely. Now we return back again up the shelled road. All at once another shell came down, we went flat as possible, but looking round we find our two pals had been hit very badly. We at once went to the rescue and found one man with his leg off. The other was dead. I knelt over the survivor and asked him if he was alright. He then said, 'Do to me what my wife would do if she was here.' I bent over him and kissed him as he passed away in my arms."

The next day was spent in clearing up the wounded as far as possible and many excursions had to be made into the open for this purpose. Another piece of description from the same pen will suffice to show "It was soon morning and we now got ready to proceed up the trenches. We went round and round, stepping over dead bodies, the sight was awful. We were also plastered with blood and mud, and the stench was appalling. At last we found ourselves in the first line trench and we had to be careful and use tact. Now we came to an opening in the trench. The N.C.O. gave us orders to be careful and go over by twos. The Germans were very quiet as we managed to carry the stretchers over. The sight was awful. Germans and British lying together in hundreds. One poor boy had been lying a long time wounded, holding his Testament in his hand. Another poor boy was so thirsty he told us he had drunk his own urine to keep himself alive."

Another man tells how the bearers of his Ambulance were taken up by Lieut. R. I. Harris, who first paraded the men and told them of the impending attack, adding it was not necessary for him to ask them to acquit themselves like men. After a hard day's work, they fell in, and in single file followed Lieut. Harris to the line. Eventually they reached what appeared to be a disused piece of trench and spent the remainder of the night there. Shells, machine gun and rifle fire passing over their heads whilst they stood there amid the din with never a chance of even sitting down for a rest. The same writer goes on to speak of the inspiring example set by Lieut. Harris, who regardless of personal danger made journeys across part of the ground gained by the infantry, lifted his man bodily and returned to his dug-out, which was temporarily arranged as an Aid Post.

Another little incident which is worth recording is that of two stretcher bearers who were returning for another case, passing on their way two cases being taken down by two pairs of 134th bearers. Just as they approached the foremost stretcher, a whizz bang came over, a splinter of which severed an artery in the leg of one of the returning men,

Private J. Wooton also of the 134th. The foremost stretcher bearer, Private L. Stokes, seeing the urgent necessity of his comrade called back to his fellow bearer to lower stretcher and immediately dived for his friend's leg, in an endeavour to stop the bleeding. Telling his mate to return for a tourniquet he held on to the leg for quite fifteen minutes, an easy prey to shell-fire. Upon the arrival of the tourniquet, it was applied and the wounded man carried to the A.D.S. Meanwhile two other bearers had carried the other case down.

The recorder of this incident also tells how he and his fellow bearers were returning empty with a stretcher when they were hailed by an infantry man asking them to go to the assistance of a man who was lying out in the open. They found, after a difficult and trying journey, the wounded man, one of the 4/5th Black Watch, in a shell hole just over the top of a ridge, with a very badly smashed leg. Setting down the stretcher they were about to lift him on when he begged them to allow him to get on it unaided. Sitting up as best he could, he lifted his wounded leg with his two hands and very gently laid it upon the stretcher first. He next lifted his body on the edge of the stretcher and then by easy stages, first his leg, then body, gradually settled himself in the middle of the canvas and lay down. When he said " right " the bearers first climbed as best they could out of the shell hole and made across some thirty yards of open as quickly as possible. Through all of which, though suffering the greatest discomfort, the wounded Scot never once " loosed a moan," an object lesson in the bearing of pain. By more easy stages he finally reached the A.D.S.

Another writes of a boy known amongst his fellows as Twick, probably hailing from Twickenham, who was the foremost bearer of a stretcher bringing in a wounded man, when he was suddenly shot through the heart by a sniper. " Poor Twick, he was very young and I shall never forget his look as he dropped, for I all but caught him."

At the close of hostilities a Communion Service was held in the surgery at Cookers when this improvised sanctuary, reeking with the sickening smell of blood, was crowded by mud-bespattered men. It was a service which bore a peculiar efficacy and a significance beyond the greatest ritual. At times the padre's voice was drowned by the noise of shell fire.

In the light of later events an entry in the War Diary by one of the O's.C. Ambulance, dated 14th September, 1916, gives room for reflection and a smile.

" Active operations by French and British are to start and it is hoped that in the succeeding days the result may be that a winter campaign will be unnecessary."

The Front now held by our Division extended from the River Ancre to Watling Street, and was held by three Brigades, each with two battalions in the line. The R.A.P's were as under:—

Right Brigade, Hamel and Knightsbridge.
Centre Brigade, Uxbridge Road, Thurles Dump.
Left Brigade, Second Avenue, White City.

OUTSKIRT FARM

DUHALLOW, A.D.S.

THE ASYLUM, YPRES.   A.D.S.

On September 6th, the 132nd Field Ambulance moved to Bertrancourt with an A.D.S. at Mailly Maillet and advanced posts at Auchonvillers and Thurles Dump. Bertrancourt was heavily shelled on more than one occasion with the result that all the Field Ambulance patients had to be carried into adjoining field for safety.

September 14th saw the main section of the Ambulance established at Bus, with an A.D.S. at Red House, and another at Colincamps, with Posts at Euston, View Post and R.A.P's at Mountjoy, Bow Street, Flag Avenue and Observatory Wood.

At this time the Ambulance was evacuating for seven battalions who were in the line at one time. On October 1st, the Division moved into the Thiepval-Courcelette Front, II Corps, Lieut.-Gen. Sir Claude W. Jacob, K.C.B., and an advance party was sent to take over the A.D.S. at Lancashire Dump, while on the 2nd, the A.D.S's at Colincamps and Red House and M.D.S. at Bertrancourt were handed over to the 5th Field Ambulance, and on the 3rd the M.D.S. at Bus was handed over to 1/2nd Highland Field Ambulance, and the Head Quarters of the 132nd Field Ambulance moved to Forceville. On October 5th, Forceville was handed to No. 1 Field Ambulance of the 63rd Naval Division, and 2 officers and 50 O.R's proceeded to Lancashire Dump, with Paisley Avenue as A.D.S. and Posts at Aveluy, Wood Post, Black Horse Bridge, Ross Castle, Lemberg Post, Thiepval. On 10th October the H.Q. of the Ambulance were established at Lancashire Dump.

F

The principal posts in the Thiepval Sector with the personnel attached to each, were as under:—

R.A.P's	Thiepval	...	...	...	17 O.R.
F.A.P's	Thiepval	...	⎫		2 Sub. Divs.
	Lemberg Post		⎬ Right		17 O.R.
	Wood Post	...	⎭		22 O.R.
	New Post	...	...Centre.		
	Johnson's Post		⎫		8 O.R.
	Ross Castle	...	⎬ Left		5 O.R.
	Barrier Post	...	⎪		
	Swallows Nest		...	...	2 O.R.
	Black Horse Bridge	...	...		4 O.R.
A.D.S's	Aveluy Post	...	...2 officers, 20 O.R.		
	Lancashire Dump		... 3 officers, 20 O.R.		
	Paisley Avenue		... 2 officers, 20 O.R.		

The chief line of evacuation for the two R.A.P's in Thiepval was by Thiepval-Authuille-Aveluy Roads from thence to the A.D.S. Left line of evacuation from R.A.P. over the open to crossroads and thence down the Valley by the East and South sides of Thiepval Wood to Paisley Avenue A.D.S. and thence by trolley to the Southern Causeway across the Ancre to Barrier Post. Thence to Lancashire Dump.

From Ross Castle down Sandy Avenue to Paisley Avenue A.D.S. and then to Lancashire Dump.

In sympathy with these many moves the 133rd Field Ambulance moved to East Clairfaye where a D.R.S. under canvas was established, they having handed over the D.R.S. at Vauchelles to the 1/3rd Highland Field Ambulance. During this move

Sir Douglas Haig and his suite passed by and after a short conversation with the O.C. Field Ambulance he proceeded to inspect the men.

The 134th Field Ambulance handed over the M.D.S. and Corps Collecting Station to the 100th Field Ambulance on the 2nd October and moved to the Cabstand on the 5th, taking over from the 56th Field Ambulance. One section being sent to C.C.S. at Contay, although the Ambulance still held Mesnil and Cookers.

These two A.D.S's, however, were handed over to the 63rd Naval Division on October 15th, and the Collecting Post at Mailly Maillet, which was taken over from the 133rd Field Ambulance on the 12th was also handed over on the 16th.

Whilst in this area Capt. Porter renewed his acquaintance with the old portion of the line in which he had served as an infantry officer before being transferred to the R.A.M.C.

Corporal F. H. Mann, of the 132nd Field Ambulance was awarded the M.M. on September 28th, by the G.O.C., V Corps, which decoration was also bestowed on Private A. Green of the 133rd Field Ambulance on September 30th, and Private J. Cullen, of the 134th Field Ambulance, on September 29th.

The 133rd Field Ambulance received orders on October 7th to open a Collecting Post at Mailly Maillet, Hotel de Ville and to man Posts at White City, Second Avenue, Thurles Dump, Sunken Road, and Auchonvillers. Whilst on the 8th, a

Collecting Post was established at Blarney and Aid Posts at Tenderloin and Spirochaete Corner. On October 9th this unit received the body of Colonel Pouks of the Russian General Staff, for burial.

In the afternoon of October 14th, the 118th Infantry Brigade attacked successfully Schwaben Redoubt. This was an oval-shaped fortification of which the Germans held half and we the remaining portion. The capture of this was an easy accomplishment but the price was paid in its retention. As soon as this was all our own the enemy poured in a constant succession of shells with obvious results to the unfortunate garrison. The 132nd Field Ambulance, reinforced by personnel from 133rd and 134th Field Ambulances was responsible for the evacuation. During this operation Lieut. S. A. Walker, M.O. in charge 1/6th Cheshire, was killed while dressing a wounded prisoner outside his Aid Post. His batman and a medical orderly were also killed. Capt. J. F. Field who was sent up as relief was blown some distance by a bursting shell and had to be sent down suffering from shell shock.

Capt. J. W. Wayte, M.O. in charge 14th Hants, was wounded and evacuated.

Private J. W. Taylor of the 133rd Field Ambulance was also wounded. During the day 151 lying cases and 418 walking cases passed through the Ambulance.

The 63rd Naval Division relieved the 39th Division in the line north of the River Ancre by noon on the 16th October.

Corporal Blaker and Private S. Walker of the 132nd Field Ambulance were wounded on October 19th and Lieut.-Colonel A. S. Williams, O.C. 133rd Field Ambulance, was evacuated sick on October 16th, Captain G. D. Robertson assuming temporary command in his place. Major C. R. Millar, the D.A.D.M.S. of the Division, was evacuated sick at this time and was succeeded by Capt. B. A. Odlum on October 26th.

A further attack by the Division was carried out on October 21st, this time the 116th Brigade having as its objective Stuff Trench. The 116th Brigade attacked with two battalions, assisted on the right by the 25th Division. The objectives were gained in a very short time and held. Again the medical arrangements were in the hands of the 132nd Field Ambulance supported by personnel from the other units. During this operation Capt. J. Rees was severely wounded and Private Trace killed whilst carrying out a reconnaissance near Mill Road. Three men of the 133rd Field Ambulance were also wounded. Privates Spall, Brown and Hughes.

A footnote from the report of the A.D.M.S. on this occasion needs no comment.

" The rapidity and success of the evacuations over such difficult and shell-torn area, under bad weather conditions and at times heavy fire, was due to the indefatigable zeal and devotion of Capt. S. Miller and Capt. L. R. Meech and the bearers."

And this, addressed to Capt. Miller from the O.C. 17th King's Royal Rifle Corps, Lieut.-Col. E. T. Wood.

"Will you please accept and convey to all ranks concerned my sincere thanks for the splendid help on the morning of the 22nd, in bringing in the wounded from the front line.

Owing to our heavy casualties and the necessity of every available man being used to hold the line, it would have been impossible to have cleared the trenches without the help of your bearers who worked magnificently under heavy shell fire and most trying conditions."

Conditions at this time were appalling. The food was of the poorest with the result that men's health suffered severely. Diarrhœa accompanied with the passing of blood was a prevalent complaint. Paisley Dump, which was beside a narrow bridge over the Ancre, and consisted of a low confined dug-out, formerly used by the French, running under a bank, was packed with men so closely they could hardly lie down for a sleep. It was practically full of vermin, the lice even dropping from the ceiling. Rats, too, were in abundance, many of whom were so fat they could barely elude capture.

Carrying under these conditions is best told by one actively engaged therein, who writes: "I had cooled down, but my clothes were still wet with my former exertions "—carrying down a wounded man—" and the night air struck chilly as we emerged from the stuffy dug-out. We were soon warm again, going over the rough ground, stumbling occasionally as our weary legs almost gave way from time to time. We reached the post on the roadway and returned. We were thoroughly weary and used up and could hardly drag our legs forward. By the time we reached the dug-out we were ready to drop from sheer fatigue. The brain felt curiously numb and one felt a hundred years old. The body craved for rest: rest and drink."

And this for a piece of description of the trenches in the Thiepval area: " The trenches were knee-deep in gluey mud and it was the hardest work I have ever done and the hardest strain I have ever experienced. The banks on each side were full of buried or half-buried corpses and the stench was appalling. As one was carrying a wounded man down one perhaps got stuck in the mud, and staggered whilst one extricated one's self or was extricated. You put out a hand to steady yourself, the earth gave way and you found you were clutching the blackened face of a half-buried German. Here and there a hand stuck out from the side and in one place a dead face looked up from the bottom of the trench, the rest of the body being buried. Mingled with the odour of putrefying flesh was always the odour of powder; a heavy, sickening stench in itself. Sometime we used to risk being shelled and got out on top."

Several writers agree that the Germans at this time had every respect for stretcher bearers engaged in their work, refraining from shelling or sniping on such occasions.

Here is a piece of description characteristic of the work. " On one occasion we had to run the gauntlet of machine gun fire when a party of us advanced over the open ground to the front line in order to collect some cases. We had some infantry helping us. We dashed about twenty yards then went down flat when the machine guns cracked. Now and again we saw the ground spit up in front of us, we were being fired at from a cross position. I should say the morning was misty and we were not visible, though could be heard by the amplifiers. We made a final dash and landed almost head first in the front trench. When we dropped they thought we had been hit. We formed a squad with three R.A.M.C. and an infantryman and began our journey down the trench. The trench was very narrow and we could only carry two at a time, and we had slightly to close the stretcher in order to make it fit our shoulders."

Another man tells how a party going in search of wounded found a dug-out full of them. They set to work dressing the worst and removing the dead, but were unable to leave the dug-out for three days as the Germans had trained machine guns on it. The food they had they managed to eke out, although water was very short. At the end of the three days the infantry advanced and the cases were able to be evacuated.

The 116th Infantry Brigade was relieved in the Redoubt Sector on the night of the 22/23rd October by the 56th Infantry Brigade of the 19th Division. In consequence of this the 132nd Field

Ambulance handed over Aveluy Post A.D.S. and the lines of evacuation through Wood Post and down the Thiepval—Authuille—Aveluy Road, together with Black Horse Bridge to the 58th Field Ambulance. This unit still retained Lancashire Dump A.D.S. as its Headquarters and continued to carry out the evacuation of the line through Paisley Avenue.

One more engagement and we were to be relieved. This time the Division was deputed to attack St. Pierre Divion and capture the Mill and the Crossing with the system of dug-outs and tunnels which were known to exist under the little village. This was accomplished successfully without much difficulty; aided by a morning mist on the 13th November, and the casualties were relatively light, numbering some 230.

The Bearer Division of the 132nd Field Ambulance assisted by all available bearers from the 133rd and the 134th, carried out the evacuation from the front line. Before the attack all the men were in readiness at the various Aid Posts and Advanced Posts. A section of 134th Field Ambulance under Lieut. R. I. Harris proceeded to Lancashire Dump on November 12th in readiness for the attack. As the battle progressed it was the intention of Lieut. Harris and his party to move forward and occupy a huge dug-out which was known to exist in the banks of the river. This proved to be a tunnel, 5 feet wide, 7 feet high, extending to an unknown length. This was captured at an early stage and was found to be full of Germans, who were taken prisoners, and equipment of all kinds. Captains Lindeman and Cooke moved forward and established R.A.P's here, but so much needed to be done ere the bearer party could occupy the place, that Lieut. Harris moved to Cookers where they were able to assist the R.N.D. who were in a mess with their evacuations. Whilst here orders were issued cancelling the move to the captured dug-out and the party returned to the Cabstand.

Great assistance was given by 50 Regimental Bearers stationed at Paisley Avenue A.D.S. and another 50 at the Cookers. A large number of unwounded German prisoners were utilised as stretcher bearers. Everyone worked with such a will that the battlefield was cleared of all wounded by 3.40 p.m. and from the A.D.S. and M.D.S. before nightfall.

In this operation the Division secured some 1,350 prisoners and was the crowning achievement of their portion of the Battle of the Somme.

This done our Division was relieved on the whole of its front by the 19th Division, exchanges being completed by 6 a.m., November 15th. The 39th Division being withdrawn to the VIII Corps area. The following letter was received by our G.O.C. from the Corps Commander on this occasion.

" To Major-Gen. G. J. Cuthbert, C.B., C.M.G., Commanding 39th Division.

Your Division is now leaving the II Corps and I wish to thank you all for the excellent work you have done since you came into the Corps and took over the line at the Schwaben Redoubt and down to the River Ancre. You have had a good deal of hard fighting, which has shown up the good qualities of your Brigades and Battalions, and the spirit and dash of the men have been most conspicuous. We shall always remember the gallant defence of the Schwaben Redoubt and the way your troops beat off counter attack after counter attack. The capture of St. Pierre Divion and the Hansa Line on the 13th instant was a splendid feat and a very fitting conclusion to the operations of your Division before leaving the II Corps. The results of that capture will be far-reaching, not only on account of the number of prisoners and material you took, but on account of the assistance you gave to the V Corps and the damaging effect on the morale of the enemy.

Will you please tell your Brigade Commanders, Battalion and Company Commanders and all ranks in the Division that their work all through has been thoroughly appreciated and that the departure of the Division is much regretted.

Success in war cannot be obtained unless all arms co-operate and work together in close combination. The many successes your Division has had is due to the untiring support you have had from the artillery which has never failed you. The calls on the Divisional Artillery have been heavy, but their response has always been prompt and efficient. Will you kindly convey to the C.R.A. of the 18th and 39th Division Artilleries, the thanks of the

II Corps for the efficient way all ranks of the gunners have ' played the game.'

(*Signed*) C. W. JACOB,
15th November, 1916.   *Lieut.-General,*
                              Commanding II Corps."

On November 15th, the 132nd Field Ambulance had the pleasure of handing over Paisley Avenue and Lancashire Dump to the 19th Division and proceeded to Warloy, whilst on the 16th, it moved again to Bretel. On November 18th the Ambulance made another acquaintance with the cattle trucks of the French railways, entraining at Doullens for the Ypres area.

Captain C. W. Bowles had assumed command of the 133rd Field Ambulance on October 26th, vice Lieut.-Col. Williams, and this Ambulance proceeded to Rue de Candas, Beauval, on 16th November. On November 18th it entrained at Candas.

Meanwhile the 134th Field Ambulance had been fully occupied and November 15th saw the Cabstand handed over to the 52nd Field Ambulance of the 19th Division, the unit proceeding to Warloy. From here Amplier was reached on the 16th and Doullens on the 18th, where the Ambulance then entrained for the north. It is understood that the senior N.C.O. distinguished himself on this occasion by reporting to the O.C., " The men are all in the train, sir, ready for marching off! "

During our stay on the Somme many new arrivals had been added to the Ambulances to replace those who had become casualties. In many respects the three units were entirely different from those which had marched through the summer days to the harvest fields of the Plains of Picardy. Yet the traditions were carried on. The testing time had come, and for the moment passed, and had not found these unfledged lads wanting in those qualities that were sought by the higher command. Certainly under the strain of those days and conditions men had grown to know each other better and friendships had been cemented which have not yet been broken.

For their work in connection with these operations it was announced later that the following awards had been made:—

M.C. to:

 Lieut. R. I. Harris, 134th Field Ambulance.

 Lieut. J. B. Dunning, M.O. in charge 13th Royal Sussex.

 Lieut. S. J. Darke, M.O. in charge 16th Rifle Brigade.

132nd Field Ambulance. M.M. to:

 65792. Sergeant A. G. Reeve.

 65880 Private E. Stevens.

 72040 Private A. L. Webb.

 65924 Private J. Abraham.

 65772 Private H. C. Neale.

 82054 Private H. King.

 55621 Private J. H. Hobson.

133rd Field Ambulance. M.M. to:

 72105 Private F. W. Clipson.

 72068 Private G. Powell.

 42441 Private G. A. Groves.

 72102 Private H. A. Runham.

 42357 Private C. Kennedy.

134th Field Ambulance. M.M. to:

64337	Sergeant J. B. Nutter.
3501	Private R. Arigho.
73365	Private W. J. Brookes.
6336	Private A. J. Taylor.
52777	Private A. Mellor.

The Somme had many memories, individual and intimate, but to one there remains the imperishable picture of a line of traffic moving over the adjoining hills, silhouetted against the amber light of the setting sun. Guns, limbers, horses, men, in a human frieze of the utmost beauty.

THE SALIENT

THE summer having proved a somewhat muddy and hectic campaign, we were pleased to arrive at the quaint and quiet villages of the Salient. It is true time proved a bad augury of this district, yet, at the period when first we made its acquaintance that oft repeated phrase was really descriptive of this portion of the line, "All quiet on the Western Front."

The Ambulances in the order of their numerical designation detrained as follows: 132nd at Houpoutre and marched to Watou taking over the Hospice; the 133rd at Esquelbecq and proceeded to Herzeele Chateau, while the 134th also from Houpoutre, marched to Wormhoudt, where they took over a Corps Rest Station and D.R.S. with one section at Bollezeele School.

If we had sought the atmosphere of pure mediævalism we could hardly have done better than concentrate on this area with its gift of romance, individuality, and its legacy of quiet and arrested development. Here, for instance, at Esquelbecq was a perfect example of the old village, cobbled street, ancient Church with its carillon, and a fine example of moated castle. Here was Flanders, the inspirer of an immortal School, and the producer of a quaint and thrifty race.

The inn and shop signs gave evidence of the gutteral language spoken and its affinity to the German. Pillow lace was made in almost every house, whilst those magnificent horses, once the pride of Flemmings and their pictures, drew with ease huge and creaking wagons over the cobbled and muddy roads. Windmills dotted the landscape and twirled their sails as though time were not. While the flail was still wielded in barns that had witnessed centuries of harvests. Flax was spun and tobacco grown as though War with its glories and sorrows was a thing unknown. Here and there were evidences of the hurried exit from that holocaust we were soon to know, in the rough hewn shanties and wooden erections that housed the homeless from Ypres. While living examples of Memling's pictures walked the streets, kept the shops and tilled the dyke-dissected fields. Van Eyck's country had to be lived in to be appreciated. Its beauty and its wealth of sunset was not necessarily for the soldier, full of strange oaths and thoughts only of his belly and his home. Those flat fields and pollarded trees were for the few rather than the many. In this area, too, we noticed the picturesque and feathery tapering masts erected for the indulgence of the National Sport of Archery in happier days than these.

On December 13th, the 132nd Field Ambulance proceeded to Proven where a D.R.S. was taken over from the 130th Field Ambulance and it was here that the first Christmas abroad was spent. The day being signalized by a good dinner and a visit from the D.M.S. Second Army.

Essex Farm, A.D.S.

The Mill, Vlamertinghe
(*Post War*)

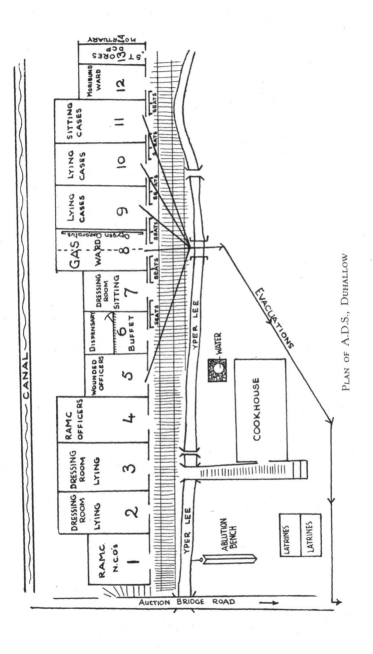

PLAN OF A.D.S., DUHALLOW

It should here be mentioned that the 39th Division had moved into the VIII Corps Reserve area on the 17th November, under Lieut.-Gen. Sir Aylmer Hunter Weston, K.C.B., D.S.O., of the Second Army under General Sir Herbert Plumer, G.C.M.G., K.C.B. Thus began a long and continuous association with this well-known and much-respected Army Commander.

While the 118th Brigade took over the Boesinghe Sector of the line, relieving the French 79th Territorial Regiment and one Battalion of the French 80th Regiment on the 29/30th November. The A.D.M.S., 38th Division, taking over R.A.P's at Boesinghe Chateau and Bluet Farm and a Collecting Post at Larry Farm. The remainder of the Division moved into the Left Sector of the VIII Corps Front on December 11th in relief of the 38th Division. We also made our first acquaintance with the famous box respirators on November 30th.

The evacuation of this portion of the line was as under. Right Sector, R.A.P., Irish Farm, R.A.P., La Belle Alliance. Left Sector, R.A.P., Morocco Farm, R.A.P., Canal Bank. Battle Aid Post, The Willows, Lancashire Farm. A.D.S., Outskirt Farm, A.D.S., Essex Farm, A.D.S., Sussex Farm.

The 133rd Field Ambulance made themselves very comfortable at Herzeele, where a particularly successful concert was held on the 9th of December. December 11th, however, proved a rather unfortunate day, for, as an Advance Party of the unit was assembling to march out, an enemy aeroplane passing overhead seizing the opportunity, dropped a bomb almost in the midst, killing Sergt. Barber, a dispenser, and wounding Privates Timms, Ealey, E. Jones, Nation, Aylett and Jolly. December 11th saw Lieut. Limbery and a party proceed to take over an A.D.S., east of Ypres, known as Outskirt Farm. Whilst on December 13th the unit moved its Headquarters to Gwent Farm on the Elverdinghe Road. December 25th was celebrated in traditional style, and a good dinner provided, consumed and, it is hoped, digested.

The 116th Infantry Brigade relieved the 115th Infantry Brigade in the Boesinghe Sector on the 30th December. This sector was held with one battalion in the line and one in support with Headquarters in Ferme de Bluet. One battalion remained in reserve with Headquarters at Ferme Cardoen. In consequence, the 133rd Ambulance opened an A.D.S. at Larry Farm on the 29th, with an R.A.P. at Boesinghe Chateau.

On December 13th, the 134th Field Ambulance proceeded to Gwalia Farm on the Elverdinghe Road, having handed over Wormhoudt to the 131st Field Ambulance and taking over the M.D.S. from the 129th Field Ambulance with A.D.S.'s at Essex and Sussex Farms, Canal Bank. An interesting case from the medical point of view was discovered on December 22nd when the unit had to deal with some cerebro-spinal suspects. It was found that the ward orderly was himself a carrier of this dread disease. He was summarily evacuated.

Christmas Day was celebrated in great style by this unit, who roasted a pig whole in a specially erected field oven. A holiday marked the event and closed by a concert, the memory of which still lingers in the minds of many. Especially the trio, one with a walking stick and tin whistle attachment, another with a couple of bones and the third with a banjo.

The A.D.M.S. appears to have been invited to all the three Field Ambulance dinners, but as his gastronomical powers were not equal to three meals of this kind in one day he declined with grace.

A battle casualty of one O.R. occurred in the personnel of the 134th on December 27th.

Work on the new A.D.S. Duhallow at Canal Bank, so named after the famous South Irish Hunt, commenced at the latter end of 1916, the material having to be fetched from Ypres. Squads worked on this night and day and a very fine Dressing Station was the result. A series of concrete dug-outs providing wards for various kinds of cases that were almost bomb proof. Whilst in occupation of this position the Prince of Wales visited these parts and was seen by large numbers of our men. The Division had thus made its acquaintance with the most famous of all the War cities, Ypres, and was to remain here longer, surely, than any other Division of the British Army.

To describe this city of the dead in any adequate manner is well-nigh impossible. One had to visit this ghost, by night and day, see for one's self, stand quietly by and let its awe inspiring atmosphere sink gradually into one's soul. It seemed at times as though the million dead had gathered themselves about the place and the air was thick with their spirits. It was as though whole pages of the old Hebrew prophets had come to life, and the severity, the doom, the vengeance of a great God had been wrought here. Streets utterly deserted, magnificent buildings razed to the ground, homes ransacked, Churches desolate. Ruined limbers and dead horses lay in the square. Men moved as quickly as possible from wall to wall, treading quietly, realising that here was no abiding place other than in tunnels under the earth or cellars. While ever and anon the shriek of shells made greater gaps in ruined walls, ploughed larger holes in pitted roads, disinterred again the broken dead, or spent themselves upon the scarred ramparts. Below the ramparts was the stagnant water of the moat, on the surface of which dead fish floated from the shells that stirred its muddy depths. Yet here, in this holocaust, were two of the finest Dressing Stations on the Western Front, one at the Prison, which was lit by electric light, where also lived the Town Mayor; and the other at the Asylum which was the first building of any size reached from the Poperinghe road. The Germans, of course, well knew that the whole of this immense Salient had to be served through this city, which was the one and only key.

1917 opened with some bitterly cold weather and heavy falls of snow followed, which lay on the ground for many weeks. The weather was of such severity that even a water cart of the 133rd Field Ambulance was frozen up and put out of action.

During January our Division was relieved in the Left Sector by the 38th Division, and in turn relieved the 55th Division in the Right Sector of the Corps Front, between the 12/17th of the month. The Brigades were now located in the Right Sector at Railway Wood and in the Left Sector at Wieltje with Headquarters at the Ramparts, Ypres. The R.A.P.'s were for the Right Sector at Railway Embankment and Potije Chateau, and the Left Sector at Potije Wood and St. Jean.

At 12 o'clock on New Year's eve a large shell was sent whistling over our lines by the Germans, evidently intended as a New Year's Gift, with best wishes.

As far as the 132nd Field Ambulance was concerned January, 1917, brought news that Private H. Everall had been Mentioned in Despatches, while later in the month Capt. J. Morris was awarded the M.C. On January 14th, this Ambulance handed over the D.R.S. at Proven to the 129th Field Ambulance and proceeded to another D.R.S. at Hillhoek, taking over from the 1/3rd West Lancs. Field Ambulance. Here amid the wintry weather the remainder of the month was spent.

January 7th was signalised by the 133rd Field Ambulance playing a memorable football match against D.A.D.O.S., whilst the next day Private J. Jones of this unit was wounded. On the 13th Lieut. Limbery and a party proceeded to take over the Asylum with R.A.P.'s at St. Jean and the Railway Embankment and Collecting Posts at Menin Road and Canal Bank. On the 14th this unit made its first acquaintance with Poperinghe, taking over the College. This was a long, rambling place, full of passages, stairs and windows without glass, and providing but little accommodation. The weather was so intensely cold during their first stay here, and the place in such bad condition, that braziers had to be lit in the cellars in order to dry and warm the building. The D.D.M.S., VIII Corps, paid a visit of inspection here at the end of the month. Some may remember the Chapel, with its organ, that adjoined this building, where the musically-minded of the Ambulance, having persuaded a colleague to act as blower, performed barcarolles upon its wheezy pipes.

It would be fitting here, perhaps, to say a few words regarding this little town of Poperinghe, more familiarly known as Pop., which was second only in importance to its more unfortunate neighbour Ypres.

If Ypres was the key of the Salient, Poperinghe was the key of Ypres, for the one main road that passed through its centre was the one and only way by which troops and transports could pass along to their destination, either Line or Restwards. Strategically, of course, it was of enormous importance, for here was the rail-head and here the centre of all this much fought-for portion of the Front. From the soldiers' point of view it was a city of refuge, where supplementary meals could be obtained and such amenities as Belgium could afford to its perforce occupants. It consisted of a handful of houses, clustering about two Churches. A Hotel de Ville, a Square, and one or two public buildings. Here, too, was Skindles and the Officers'

Club; with Canteens of varying degrees of efficiency. And, above all, that remarkable institution born of the War, known as Talbot House, and now happily surviving as Toc H. Who can forget its comfortable walls, the books that lined its shelves, the original notices that adorned its welcome, and, not least, the celebrated hotelier, the Rev. P. B. Clayton, who presided over its destinies and made it a centre of life to so many whose life was death? And there are those who would remember the Chapel, tucked away under its roof, where one could kneel before the Carpenter's Bench and be translated out of all the chaos that raged in the adjoining fields. A beautifully-furnished Sanctuary, where candles dimly lit its richness and the mud-stained boots and clothing of those who there sought worship.

Poperinghe was, of course, shelled very considerably by long range guns, for the Germans were not unmindful of its importance, the rail-head being a specially sought-out target for these occasions. More than once the leave train, waiting here, was hit and poor fellows instead of proceeding home were carried into adjoining hospitals or mortuaries. In order to lessen congestion and consequent risks our engineers had thrown a switch road about the town, which in turn came in for a good deal of attention from enemy gunners. The Town Hall abutted on to the main road on the outskirts of the town nearest Ypres and here was displayed the famous sign, "Wind Safe" or "Wind Dangerous." Between Poperinghe and Ypres was that famous or infamous, stretch of cobbled tree-lined road that led straight through

Vlamertinghe, along which all troops and transports must pass. The throbbing, clattering stream that ever passed and turned this quiet rural district into one of the busiest thoroughfares night and day. At this time of our advent it seemed the main artery of the War. Guns, limbers, G.S. wagons, steaming kitchens, ration carts, ammunition wagons followed unceasingly along its way. Whilst engineers were busy laying railways, throwing bridges and ever pushing more lines of communication into the very mouth of Hell.

On January 13th, 1917, the 134th Field Ambulance handed over Essex and Sussex Farms to the 38th Division and took over the Prison, A.D.S. at Ypres, with Collecting Posts at Potije Wood and St. Jean. Potije Post consisted of a passage-shaped shelter, about 15 feet by 6 feet, constructed of sandbags and covered with pit props and sand bags, while Potije Chateau comprised two rooms under the original roof. The Dressing Room was unprotected except on the east side. The R.A.P. in Potije Wood was a covered passage, very dark and narrow, reached by trench-boards through the Wood.

On the 14th the Headquarters of the unit moved to Gwent Farm on the Elverdinge Road taking over from the 2/1st West Lancs Field Ambulance. On the 16th B section of this unit took over L'Ebbe Farm on the outskirts of Poperinghe. The long tree-lined approach from the road, of this rural retreat, some foot deep in thick mud, may be recalled by some who sojourned here, and the plentiful supply of hot water that could be obtained from this Farm which was also a tobacco factory.

The first three months of the year were uneventful as far as the whole Division was concerned. We seemed to spend the time making an acquaintance with every portion of the area. A raid was carried out by the 16th Rifle Brigade on the night of February, 14/15th, directed against the Mound, situated 800 yards north of Gheluvelt. This proved abortive as the Mound was strongly held. This was followed by another by the 1/1st Herts. The evacuation on the occasion of the raid by the 16th Rifle Brigade was as follows:—

Left Sector via Barnsley Road over Bridge 60 to the R.A.P., thence to Sussex Farm A.D.S. Centre Sector transferred to R.A.M.C. Bearers in hutments at head of Skipton Road Trench, from thence by Skipton Trolley Line over Bridge 6.

Right Sector, down Skipton Road leaving flooded trench for duckboards, over Bridge 6 W. to R.A.P. The two A.D.S., Sussex and Essex Farms, were under the charge of Capt. Gatchell, S.M.O., Canal Bank. Motor Ambulances then cleared from A.D.S. to the M.D.S. via Salvation Corner, Reigersburg Chateau, Brielen and Elverdinghe. Walking wounded proceeded from A.D.S. to Brielen through Austerlitz Farm.

The 55th Division relieved our own in the Right Divisional Sector and we accordingly moved into VIII Corps Reserve area. And on the 27th February, our Division moved into the X Corps, Lieut.-Gen. Sir T. L. Morland, K.C.B., K.C.M.G., D.S.O., taking over from the 23rd

Division. In consequence of these Divisional moves the 132nd Field Ambulance vacated Proven on the 17th February and established itself at Wormhoudt where it functioned another D.R.S., this time with a Field Ambulance site as well, and a C.R.S. for officers. On the 22nd parties of this Ambulance took over baths, and laundries at Poperinghe, Ypres and Winnipeg Camp. While on the 27th the Headquarters of the unit moved to Steenvoorde.

As far as the 133rd Field Ambulance was concerned, February 11th saw Capt. Sinclair Miller, M.C., assume temporary command of the unit, whilst the raid carried out by the 1/1st Herts on the 12th was served by the Ambulance. The evacuation from the line on this occasion was as follows:—

Left Sector via Barnsley Road over Bridge 6D to R.A.P., thence by wheeled stretcher to Sussex Farm A.D.S. Centre Sector, from bearers to hutment at Skipton Road trench, thence by Skipton Trolley Line to Sussex Farm. Right Sector, down Skipton Road and over Bridge 6W. The bridges mentioned were those over the Yser Canal, all of which bore numbers and special demolition arrangements for blowing them up at a moment's notice in the event of a sudden retirement. The 15th of the month saw Capt. A. W. Dennis assume temporary command, vice Capt. S. Miller, while on the 16th the Ambulance moved to Watou taking over from the 1/3rd West Lancs Field Ambulance. On the 18th Lieut.-Col. Bowles returned to his command.

On the 26th the Ambulance moved to Vlamertinghe Mill and made its first acquaintance with this famous spot on the road between Poperinghe and Ypres. The beautiful Church here adjacent was in ruins, while the little cemetery under its shadow, grew all too full. Here buried, too, was one of the first V.C's of the War, Capt. Grenfell. Quite a large amount of work was carried out at the Mill in preparation for subsequent attacks and the consequent influx of patients. It was, too, whilst in occupation of this area later, that mustard gas was first used, and although bathing used to take place in the canal, this was subsequently forbidden owing to the risk of contamination. Lt.-Col. Bowles was again evacuated sick on the 28th. The month closed with this Ambulance taking over the Bund A.D.S., with Collecting Posts at Cow Farm and Lille Gate, and R.A.P. at Zillebeke and a Relay Post at Stafford Street.

The Bund at Zillebeke consisted of a series of dug-outs constructed in the bank of Zillebeke lake, and was a very lively spot. The Dressing Station was at the corner and somewhat exposed. During our occupancy the enemy registered a direct hit on this, partially blowing it in and causing some consternation amongst those who were inside. Although we sustained no casualties here it was later learned that the Dressing Station had been blown in and the whole staff killed. Here also was the well-known and well-named Chinese Wall.

The 134th Field Ambulance moved to a Field Ambulance site at Herzelle on the 17th February, whilst a Field Ambulance site and a D.R.S. were taken over from the 69th Field Ambulance at

Waratah Camp on the 27th. Here much work was carried out in making the place habitable, the details of which are best remembered by those who laboured on the various offices. The Ambulance remained here for the best portion of two months. March came with its variable weather and witnessed the taking over on the 4th by the 132nd Field Ambulance of the Second Army Rest Station, at the famous and unique Convent des Trappistes at Mont des Cats. This Convent is situated on the last of a spur of hills which run from Ypres towards Hazebrouck, consisting of Mont Rouge and Noir, Kemnel Hill, etc. The ridge is particularly noticeable as one travels towards Ypres. It is the only bit of rising ground or series of humps in this otherwise so flat area. Mont des Cats, crowned by its convent looks particularly picturesque, like some almost fairy city. The convent was eventually destroyed by fire during the German Advance of 1918 but has since been rebuilt, and delights the traveller's eye as he proceeds by slow motion from Hazebrouck on the State Railway.

Private H. Everall of this unit was awarded the Bronze Medal for military valour by H.M. the King of Italy, on March 15th, whilst on the 31st the Divisional Commander, Major-Gen. Cuthbert visited the Rest Station and made a tour of inspection. March 1st saw Private Dye of the 133rd Field Ambulance wounded at Lille gate, whilst on March 29th, Capt. J. S. Manford, T.F., assumed command of the Ambulance vice Lieut.-Col. Bowles who had been evacuated, and on this day the Ambulance opened a Corps Collecting Post at Brandhoek.

April saw the 23rd Division return to the command of the X Corps and take over part of the line held by our Division. In consequence of this our Division extended its front from Menin Road to St. Peter's Trench. On the 16th of this month the 132nd Field Ambulance handed over Mont des Cats to the 69th Field Ambulance and moved to a D.R.S. at Proven, which was taken over from the 129th Field Ambulance. Whilst on the same day the 133rd Field Ambulance again returned to the College at Poperinghe, also taking over Essex Farm A.D.S. at Canal Bank, which was described as one of the cleanest places that we were ever called upon to man, with its Collecting Post at Outskirt Farm from the 130th Field Ambulance.

The 20th saw the telephone installed to the unit, which was hailed by the O.C. as a great asset. It also showed how stationary the War had become and how everything was settling down into a series of ordered events. We took over the line, vacated and rested as though it were some new form of business. Lieut. and Qr. Master Curling of this unit was evacuated sick on the 24th and some days later news was received of his death. Thus passed one whom the Ambulance had learned to respect and appreciate for his cheery and genial presence.

The 134th Field Ambulance accomplished two moves in this month. One to Bollezelle on the 16th and to Watou on the 28th.

Some may recall a rather jealous barber at Watou who had a young and pretty wife. Customers had to wait their turn in an ante-room and whilst so doing were pleased to pass the time of day with madame. The barber could hear all that was said and too often became so excited that his antics whilst shaving a man, were alarming. Razor in one hand he would dance about in an endeavour to see what was going on with his wife in the adjoining room.

May was significant by reason of the 132nd Field Ambulance holding a Sports' Meeting for the Division on the 9th, when the A.D.M.S. was the chief judge. The other two judges being found in the A.D.V.S. and the O.C. Divisional Train, A.S.C. This was a large meeting, greatly appreciated by all who took part, and brought to a successful conclusion on a very nice day. The D.D.M.S., VIII Corps, was also present. The 132nd Field Ambulance was awarded the first prize for G.S. wagons and Water Cart turn out; the second for the riding pony and the third for the Ambulance Wagon. In the open events the quarter-mile flat race went to the 132nd, the 100 yards to the 4th M.A.C. and the half-mile to the 46th C.C.S. Notification was also received on the 30th that Sergeant-Major B. G. Sharpe of this unit was Mentioned in Despatches.

Work in the Line proceeded as usual during May for the 133rd Field Ambulance and a sad incident occurred at the Asylum on the 12th, when a direct hit, in a peculiar manner, was registered on the Dressing Station there. A shell came down the back stairs, killing 4 O.R. and wounding 2 O.R., the whole of the Staff. Their names were:

88007 Private A. C. Caunt.

90749 Private W. M. Timson.

61515 Private D. L. Boyle.

72048 Private H. Tillyard (died on arrival at C.C.S.)

65127 S/Sergeant J. H. Smith.

69593 Private A. B. Clarke.

Poperinghe was shelled on two or three days during this month, many shells falling in close proximity to the College, rendering it almost untenable. Therefore it was with some relief that the Ambulance moved to the Cloisters on the 13th, finding this a much more suitable place for a Field Ambulance, with its better accommodation. It was, however, in a very dirty condition and much work had to be expended in order to make it fit for habitation.

May 5th saw the 134th Field Ambulance establish a Collecting Post at Bayenghem lez Seninghem and on the 15th this Field Ambulance was moved to the Red Chateau, Poperinghe. From here on the 17th, Capt. R. I. Harris and a party took over the new A.D.S. at Canal Bank, Duhallow, which the 133rd Field Ambulance was constructing, and work on this was carried a further stage. On the 30th of the month it was notified that the A.D.M.S., Lieut.-Col. Hildreth, Capts. Huggins and Porter were all Mentioned in Despatches.

Although these months seem uneventful from the chronicle point of view, yet work of one kind and another was being pushed forward in anticipation of severe fighting to come. The Germans were not unmindful of this. Their balloons, which could be seen in the Salient as clearly as our own, were ever watchful of this activity behind our lines. Hence the frequent and persistent shelling of both forward and back areas which was taking place, and the continued attacks, often successfully, of our balloons. These latter exploits by enemy airmen and the consequent sudden burst of anti-aircraft fire and parachute displays enlivened the scene many days in the week. Guns of varying calibre were being pushed forward by huge cater-pillar tractors or on railways; and ammunition dumps erected by the roadside that spoke volumes for those who realised the import of such phenomena.

The offensive actually opened in June when Messines ridge was captured, Hill 60 being blown up by the engineers. Our own offensive, however, was not due until July. In preparation for this the 39th Division was transferred to the XVIII Corps, Lieut.-Gen. Sir F. I. Maxse, K.C.B., C.V.O., D.S.O., of the Fifth Army, on June 10th, and the following messages were received from the Army and Corps Commanders:—

"VIII Corps,

9th June, 1917.

To Major-General G. J. Cuthbert, C.B., C.M.G., Commanding 39th Division.

The Army Commander (General Sir Herbert Plumer, G.C.M.G., K.C.B.), wishes me to express his regret at the departure of the VIII Corps and of the 39th Division from his command.

He wishes to assure you and your staff and all Commanders and troops who have been acting under you, that he thoroughly appreciates the excellent work that has been done by them all during the time they have served with the Second Army. He wishes them to feel that he is fully satisfied with the standard of efficiency they have attained. He is confident that your fine Division will carry out successfully any tasks assigned to them, and he wishes you all the best of luck.

(*Signed*) Aylmer Hunter Weston,
Lieut.-General,
Commanding VIII Corps "

" From Lieut.-Gen. Sir Aylmer Hunter Weston, K.C.B., D.S.O., M.P.

To the Officers, Warrant Officers, N.C.O.'s and Men of the 39th Division.

To my great regret the development of the Military situation necessitates your leaving my command.

During the time that the Division has been in my Corps all ranks from General to Private have done splendid service to the State. It has been a privilege and a pleasure to me to have the 39th Division under my command, and I much hope that it may be my good fortune to serve with you again.

Aylmer Hunter Weston,
June, 1917.   *Lieut.-General.*"

The 132nd Field Ambulance began to dismantle the D.R.S. at Proven on the 13th June, which job having been accomplished they moved to Herzeele on the 20th where A and B Sections erected a C.R.S.

Poperinghe came in for a good deal of attention from enemy gunners at this time and on June 19th the R.E. yard there, not far from the Cloisters, was heavily shelled and many casualties resulted. These were attended to by the 133rd Field Ambulance. Whilst on the 23rd the unit again took over Duhallow A.D.S. relinquishing in turn Essex Farm. Capt. Meech was wounded and evacuated on the 25th and 2 O.R.'s were killed and 2 O.R.'s wounded, attached from the 134th Field Ambulance at the same time. On the 29th the unit proceeded to Gwent Farm, while work still progressed at Duhallow.

The Canal Bank was a hive of industry at this time. Dumps of various kinds of shells had been established, whilst battery positions jostled one another the whole way along. It was inevitable that the enemy should succeed in finding some of these positions. On one such occasion our men were called upon to clear up the gunners. The guns and teams were alike knocked out, one poor youth of eighteen having been blown across the road into a ditch opposite. He was badly wounded and died on the way to the A.D.S. Many of the dumps were blown up exploding with such force that the whole of the series of dug-outs rocked. The Red Hart Estaminet, with its contents, went up on one memorable occasion. Another rather fiery incident was when a train-load of trucks caught fire here and was destroyed.

June commenced with the 134th Field Ambulance by Chateau Rouge being shelled on the 7th, and the patients there had to be carried to positions of safety. Even this had its amusing side as the hospital at this time was fairly full of trench feet cases, some rather bad. The shelling had an extraordinary healing effect as many of these men had been unable to put their feet to the ground, but on the advent of the shells were seen to be scampering off in all directions, their feet swathed in bandages and cotton wool. It was, however, a painful duty of one of the orderlies to climb to the top of an adjacent building and remove a limb which had belonged to one of the patients who had not been quick enough to get away.

On the 11th a car orderly of this unit was wounded at Duhallow, which had become a somewhat unhealthy spot. Reconstruction of the R.A.P. at La Belle Alliance was also carried out by a working party. Chateau Rouge was relinquished on the 19th and the Ambulance parked, whilst on the 21st C Section of this unit proceeded on a summer holiday to Salperwick, near St. Omer. The 25th saw the unit moved to Gwalia Farm, which was a little higher up the Elverdinghe Road than Gwent Farm, and there preparations were made for the establishment of a Corps Main Dressing Station. Towards the end of the month, on the night of the 22/23rd June to be exact, the 51st Highland Division, less artillery, took over the left Sector of the XVIII Corps Front from our Division. June saw the D.S.O. conferred on Lieut.-Col. A. S. Littlejohns of the 132nd Field Ambulance and Lieut.-Col. H. C. Hildreth of the 134th Field Ambulance, which two officers were also Mentioned in Despatches, together with Capts. J. H. Porter, W. T. Brown, R. C. Cooke, G. W. Huggins and A. E. Delgado.

July was the commencement of active operations as far as our Division was concerned, and in anticipation of this, the 132nd Field Ambulance handed over the C.R.S. at Herzeele to the 35th Field Ambulance on the 20th and moved to Gwalia Farm on the 21st to the C.M.D.S. which had been established there by the 134th Field Ambulance. The 132nd Field Ambulance being responsible for a Walking Wounded Collecting Post.

Meanwhile the 133rd Field Ambulance remained with its Headquarters at Gwent Farm. An unfortunate incident occurred here when a shell struck the gable end of the barn, killing one, Private Lock, and wounding 2 O.R.'s. On the 19th, Capt. Mansfield of this unit was evacuated gassed, while on the 29th, the personnel for the A.D.S. and the bearer division were sent up the line. On the way up Corporal Windsor was killed and one O.R. wounded.

The 134th Field Ambulance was heavily shelled on the 8th, the site being temporarily evacuated in consequence, and on the 24th C-section returned from their rustication in the back area; one A.S.C. H.T. Sergt. dying en route of heart trouble. On the 25th the 1/2nd Highland Field Ambulance of the 51st Division arrived at the C.M.D.S. to assist, as this Division, with our own, comprised the two attacking Divisions of the XVIII Corps front.

The Passchendaele operations, or Third Battle of Ypres, commenced at 3.31 a.m. on the morning of the 31st July, after an intense bombardment, the XVIII Corps, consisting of four Divisions, attacking on the Corps Front from Spree Farm to

Hurst Park, with two Divisions in the line and two in reserve. The Division working in pairs, the 39th and 48th on the right, and the 51st and 11th on the left. The 39th and 51st being the attacking Divisions. In readiness the A.D.S. Duhallow had been manned by the various bearer sub-divisions of the Ambulances. Two bearers were told off to each Battalion to act as runners between R.A.P.s and D.C.P. and all ranks were at their various stations three hours before the attack opened. A Divisional Collecting Post had been established near Hammonds Corner, in the neighbourhood of St. Jean, which acted as the Headquarters of the O.C. Bearers, Capt. Warwick. The personnel were disposed as under :

D.C.P., 2 officers, 60 O.R.
La Brique Post, 1 N.C.O., 10 O.R.
Left R.A.P., 10 Bearers | neighbourhood of
Right R.A.P., 10 Bearers | Forward Cottage.
La Belle Alliance, 1 N.C.O., 10 Bearers.
Wilson Farm, 2 N.C.O.'s, 59 Bearers.
La Brique Village, 1 N.C.O., 20 Bearers.

The remainder at Duhallow A.D.S., which was under the charge of Capt. G. D. Robertson.

During the morning Duhallow came in for some shelling and the end dug-out was hit, wounding a German prisoner. The D.C.P. had a busy time, some 1,000 cases passing through during the day. German Prisoners being used to convey many of the stretcher cases to the A.D.S.

All went well for the first few hours and a steady stream of wounded came in from the line. Rain began to fall in the afternoon which soon made the ground a perfect quagmire, resulting in the necessity of six to eight men to a stretcher. Bearers had been told off to the various R.M.O.'s to act as runners and events moved so rapidly that in one instance the R.A.P. was actually in advance of the Battalion, and was thus established in No Man's Land. A large number of infantry had been ear-marked and attached to the O.C. A.D.S., but owing to a lack of control, no officer or N.C.O.'s accompanying them, they proved very unsatisfactory. Only about half could be found to carry on the work and these discovered the carrying so difficult that in many cases they could only make one journey and were then exhausted, whereas the R.A.M.C. bearers had to make five or six. Capt. Porter relieved Capt. Warwick at the D.C.P. on August 2nd at 11.30 a.m.

The following were mentioned as having done conspicuously good work:—

44914   Sergt. F. Hanson, 134th F.A.
65938   Sergt. C. Earl, 133rd Field Ambulance.
72020   L/Corpl. W. J. Drinkwater, 133rd F.A.
72155   Private W. Budd, 133rd F.A.

and Lieut. J. N. Worcester, medical reserve, U.S.A., who had shown great zeal and energy under strange and new surroundings.

Capt. Sinclair Miller took charge of the car loading post and did excellent service.

Capt. Limbery and S/Sergt. Williams worked night and day.

A good sprinkling of wounded Germans were handled on this occasion and one man brought in had been lying out for several days with his arm off. He had himself applied two tourniquets very tightly upon the stump. He asked for water and upon being given this murmured his thanks in French. His wet clothes were taken off and he was put on a clean dry stretcher and speedily evacuated. The 133rd Field Ambulance under Lt.-Col. Manford was responsible for the evacuation of the wounded on this occasion and their report as recorded in the War Diary makes pitiable reading. Owing to the appalling conditions of the ground the wounded were being brought in in a greatly exhausted state, the bearers also being worn out as the carry in many cases was 2½ miles from St. Julien.

The road from Hammonds Corner to the A.D.S. became very bad and the horsed ambulances that were used here were continually being bogged. While the larger motor ambulance cars in some cases took as long as two hours on the journey down. This was partly due to congestion and partly due to the condition of the road.

A large amount of supplies in the shape of stretchers, blankets, water, matches, cigarettes, rum and whisky had been sent up the line and deposited in various places such as disused trenches in readiness for the operations.

By mid-day after zero hour on the first morning 280 wounded had passed through the A.D.S. And on the third, after a series of lamentations, in the Diary, occurs this passage, which speaks for itself. " Rain still falling, conditions of bearers becoming worse, can hardly do any more journeys." And the M.O. in charge 17th K.R.R.C., reports on this day also, " No bearers have reached my R.A.P. to-day."

The casualties amongst our units were as follows: Capt. B. M. Hunter, M.O. in charge 1/1st Cambs., killed, 1/8/17. Capt. J. B. Charles, M.O. in charge 1/1st Herts, wounded, 31/7/717. Capt. D. J. MacDougal, M.O. in charge 13th Royal Sussex, wounded, 2/8/17. Capt. Rixon, M.O. in charge 16th Notts and Derbys, wounded.

132nd Field Ambulance. Killed, Private McCollins; wounded, Privates Welfare, Webb, Hall and Shrine. 133rd Field Ambulance. Killed, Corpl. Windsor; wounded, Privates Bates, Thompson, Bradwell, Keppy, Fry, Barrett, Burridge and Private Clipson, gassed.

134th Field Ambulance. Killed, Driver Belfield, A.S.C.H.T.; wounded, Privates Large, Chapman, Bradley, Bolton, Leatherdale, Leech, Morris and L/Corpl. Stokes.

On the 5th, Capt. Anderson, M.O. in charge 16th Notts and Derby was wounded.

The report of the A.D.M.S. on this, the Third Battle of Ypres, which lasted as far as we were concerned from July 31st until the Division was relieved on the night of the 5/6th August, is as follows:—

" I may state that the work in this area was carried out under the most trying conditions. The elements of long hand carriage, hostile shelling, bad going and drenching rain contrived to make the evacuation from our front line one of the most difficult to be imagined, and it was rendered possible only by courage, perseverance and devotion to duty by all ranks concerned. . . . There was no rest for these men till all our wounded within the area held by the Division were evacuated."

It should be noted that the A.D.S. Duhallow was taxed to its utmost for the first 24 hours, where a staff of five medical officers were on continuous duty, night and day. As the advance progressed, the evacuation of wounded became more difficult from the newly-established R.A.P's. In many cases the medical supplies of R.M.O.'s were completely destroyed by shell fire and most of the medical assistance had to be rendered in the open. The casualties handled by the Ambulance during the engagement were: 94 officers and 2,586 O.R.'s: In a message to the Division, the Army Commander, General Sir Hubert Gough, told us that we had done well, the Division capturing over 1,000 prisoners, more than any other Division of the British Army.

The A.D.M.S. issued the following special order, " The A.D.M.S., 39th Division, wishes to express his appreciation of the excellent work he witnessed since zero hour by Officers, N.C.O.'s and men of the R.A.M.C., both at the A.D.S., Duhallow, and the D.C.P., and he tenders his personal thanks to all ranks for the thoroughness with which they carried out their arduous duties under most difficult and trying conditions."

On the 2nd August, the A.D.M.S. sent a letter to the Div. Gen., asking that the infantry might be relieved.

The following Special Order was also issued by the A.D.M.S. on this occasion:

" SPECIAL ORDER.—Be pleased to convey to all ranks my great appreciation of the good services rendered during recent operations, both at the Advanced Dressing Station and Divisional Collecting Post under exceptional adverse circumstances.

The arduous and unselfish devotion of the bearers of each Field Ambulance, under most trying conditions, merit the highest praise.

All concerned, including the Medical Officers in charge of units, more than maintained the highest traditions of the Corps.

I desire that this special order be read out on parade to each Field Ambulance.

(Signed) G. W. Brazier-Creagh,

Colonel.

H.Q., 39th Div.   A.D.M.S., 39th Division."
    3/8/17.

The Division now came out for a well-earned though short-lived rest, having been relieved in the line on the night of the 5/6th August, by the 48th Division. The Division was now transferred to X Corps, Lieut.-Gen. Sir T. L. Morland, K.C.B., K.C.M.G., D.S.O., Second Army, under General Sir Herbert Plumer, G.C.M.G., K.C.B.

In consequence of this the 132nd Field Ambulance sent Lieut. A. Brown with a party of bearers to the 48th Divisional Field Ambulances for temporary duty, whilst the unit itself struck camp and proceeded to Meteren to a Field Ambulance site. The transport of this unit proceeded to the new area by road, whilst the personnel travelled by train.

From here on the 12th Capt. Sinclair Miller and a party of bearers proceeded to Voormezeele.

The O.C. 133rd Field Ambulance, Lieut.-Col. Manford, was evacuated sick on the 7th August, and on this day the unit moved from Gwent Farm to Caestre Station, proceeding by train to the Meteren area. This was a pleasant district, reminiscent of the very early days of the struggle, for hand-to-hand fighting had taken place here in 1914 as the lonely, individual graves bore witness. A land of quiet fields, tree-lined roads, and hop gardens, almost suggestive of Kent, while in the straggling village, the blacksmith made cheerful sparks fly from his ancient smithy and rural folks shuffled their wooden sabots about the cobbled street. Not for long, however, were the 133rd destined to remain and Chippewa Camp was reached on the 14th. Here a large amount of work was commenced in making this a Corps Main Dressing Station, with all the necessary offices of such an institution. On the 31st of the month notification was received that the Military Medal had been conferred on the undermentioned men for bravery in the Field:

65775	Sergt. F. W. Loakes,	132 F.A.
44157	Private S. Meredith,	133rd F.A.
88053	Private V. H. Keppy,	133rd F.A.
63252	Private J. L. I. Marston,	133rd F.A.
65938	Sergt. C. Earl,	133rd F.A.
65994	Private T. Eustace,	133rd F.A.
72277	A/Sergt. E. A. Cradduck,	134th F.A.
45012	Private J. H. Bradley,	134th F.A.
72130	Private T. Taylor,	134th F.A.
74443	Sergt. C. H. Searle,	134th F.A.

As far as the 134th Field Ambulance was concerned the main body moved by train to Eecke. From here a bearer division under Capt. R. I. Harris proceeded to Voormezeele, taking over from the 138th Field Ambulance on the 12th August.

The Division returned to the line on the night of the 13/14th August, relieving the 41st Division in the Front which extended from Hollebeke to Klein Zillebeke. The 116th Infantry Brigade took over from the 122nd Infantry Brigade in the Sector, Forret Farm to Ypres—Comines Canal on this date, whilst the 117th Infantry Brigade relieved the 124th Infantry Brigade on the night 14/15th, taking over from Ypres-Comines Canal to Zwarteleen Klein Zillebeke Road. The 118th Brigade remaining in reserve in Ridge Wood. Our Division was again relieved in the line on or about August 29th. The A.D.S. on this front was at the Brasserie, with a Collecting Post at Norfolk Bridge and an R.A.P. in a Pill Box at Battle Wood.

On the 17th of this month Capt. R. I. Harris was wounded, 1 O.R., Private Stanford, was killed and 19 others wounded of whom one, Private Davey, died of wounds. The total casualties for the month being 1 killed and 25 wounded of the 134th Field Ambulance. Our Division returned to the line again on the night of the 2/3rd September, when it relieved the 24th Division on the front which extended from Graveyard Cottage to the S.E. corner of Bodmin Copse, Shrewsbury Forest Sector. News was also received early in the month that the following awards had been gained for the medical services.

Bar to D.S.O., Major J. S. Y. Rogers, M.O. in charge 4/5th Royal Highlanders.
M.C., Capt. W. T. Brown,
M.C., Capt. H. J. de Brent.
Bar to M.C., Capt. R. I. Harris.
D.C.M., 72320 A/Cpl. H. Tallon.

During this period Major-Gen. G. J. Cuthbert, C.B., C.M.G., returned to England to train a Division there and Major-Gen. E. Feetham, C.B., C.M.G., assumed command in his stead.

On September 12th, the Collecting Post which had been established at Steenvoorde by the 132nd Field Ambulance, was closed. A bearer division was sent to assist the 134th Field Ambulance at the Brasserie on the 17th and on the 23rd a Main Dressing Station for lightly wounded was taken over at La Clytte and handed over to the 21st Division on the 28th September.

A new feature of the War had developed at this time in aircraft activity by the enemy. He conceived the idea, and with characteristic German thoroughness carried it out, of bombing us night and morning, between lights, each and every day as the moon and weather permitted. It certainly assumed alarming proportions as the machines seemed to come over in relays, and at times fairly shovelled out the bombs. That more damage was not done and a greater loss of life sustained is to be most wondered at. To counteract this, of course, a large amount of work had to be carried out in revetting tents, huts and horse lines, and the digging of trenches in which the personnel could take refuge.

The 133rd Field Ambulance carried out a large amount of work at Chippewa Camp, during September and were visited by enemy bombers in the vicinity several times during the month. On the 8th the A.D.M.S. held an investiture at the H.Q. of this unit and bestowed the ribbons of the awards to the various men of this Field Ambulance who had won the coveted decorations. The 10th of the month saw Capt. Limbery and 2 N.C.O.'s proceed to the 134th Field Ambulance to make a reconnaissance of the forward area, and on the 12th 10 O.R.'s proceeded to the 134th also to form a working party at the D.C.P., Zwarteleen. Capt. Sinclair Miller, M.C., was officially appointed to command 133rd Field Ambulance on the 15th of the month. Whilst on the 19th Capt. Limbery, 2 Sergeants and 72 O.R. proceeded to the 134th Field Ambulance for the active operations which commenced on the morrow.

The 134th Field Ambulance was responsible for the work in the line at this time and September 1st was signalised by Advanced Posts being taken over from the 72nd Field Ambulance at Compton Corner, Canada Street and Larch Wood. Corporal Tallon of this unit was decorated with the ribbon of the D.C.M. by the A.D.M.S. on September 5th, while on the 12th work was carried out on the D.C.P. at Zwarteleen. The 117th Infantry Brigade relieved the 118th Infantry Brigade in Ridge Wood on September 11th.

Active operations commenced at 5.40 a.m. on the morning of the 20th, when the X Corps, Second Army, attacked. Our Division was represented by the 117th Infantry Brigade in the line, with the 118th Infantry Brigade in close support at Larch Wood, Zwarteleen, and the 116th Infantry Brigade in reserve in the Millekruisse area. The objective was Bulgar Wood which was gained and the captured line held. The 19th Division, IX Corps attacked on the right and the 41st Division, X Corps, on the left.

The various medical posts were manned as under: R.A.P. at Sunken Road, with Relay Post at Trolley Railhead, Mount Sorrel Divisional Collecting Post for lying wounded at Zwarteleen, and for walking wounded at Spoil Bank, and the A.D.S. at the Brasserie. The personnel were distributed as follows : R.A.P. at Sunken Road, 2 R.M.O.'s, Capt. K. Limbery and 48 bearers. First Relay Post: 1 N.C.O. and 9 men. Railhead, Mount Sorrel: O.C. Bearers, Capt. H. D. Field, and 36 men. Subsidiary Relay Post : 1 N.C.O. and 8 men. Zwarteleen D.C.P., Capt. W. T. Brown and 45 Reserve Bearers. D.C.P. for lying wounded, Zwarteleen, Capt. J. H. Porter in charge, Capt. F. W. Stone, Capt. A. C. Murray. Coffee Stall at Corner House.

The evacuation was a difficult one, but owing to excellent reconnaissance which had been previously carried out by the officers concerned, the ground was thoroughly understood. Consequently the wounded were speedily cleared and began to arrive at the 134th Field Ambulance very early. The front line evacuation was particularly rapid, 32 officers and 540 O.R.'s passing through the A.D.S. As far as the 133rd Field Ambulance was concerned, by 11 o'clock the rate of admissions reached their maximum point, but at no time was there any congestion. Seven hundred and seventy cases of lying wounded were passed through in 24 hours which increased to 1,000 cases in 48 hours. The ground was reported clear on the evening of the 21st. On the 22nd another 13 officers and 139 O.R.'s were passed through. One very helpful feature was the addition of 200 Infantry Bearers with 4 officers who had been attached the day previously and were thus able to be instructed in the work. The number of serious cases on this occasion was very noticeable.

The A.D.M.S. reported that the magnificent courage and energy displayed by the R.A.M.C. bearers, by their devotion and gallantry, gained the praise of the combatant branches of the Division. He concluded his report by saying: " It is a pleasure to report on the fine example displayed by officers of the R.A.M.C. engaged right from the front line to the A.D.S. They vied with each other in their efforts to discharge to the utmost their onerous duties, and their fine spirit had its reward in the satisfactory completion of operations."

The A.D.M.S. was present on the battleground from zero hour and remained all day visiting the various posts.

Our Division was relieved in the Shrewsbury Forest Sector on September 23rd and took over the Tower Hamlets Sector.

The 134th Field Ambulance handed over Zwarteleen and Spoil Bank on the 24th to a Field Ambulance of the 19th Division and moved their Headquarters to Voormezeele, taking over posts from the 140th Field Ambulance. At 2 p.m., on September 25th one of the dug-outs was blown in and three bearers were killed, Privates Price, Squires and Forbes.

September 26th saw active operations again commence when the Division attacked at 5.50 a.m., the objective being the Tower Hamlets Ridge. The attack was carried out by the 118th Infantry Brigade on the right and the 116th Infantry Brigade on the left.

The 134th Field Ambulance was responsible for evacuation from the line with its Headquarters at Voormezeele and the A.D.S. at Lock 8. The Divisional Collecting Post was at Larch Wood and Advanced Collecting Posts at Hedge Street for Left Brigade, Canada Street for the Right Brigade, Capt. Warwick being in charge of Lock 8. The 33rd Division supported our left, whilst a Brigade of the 37th Division covered the right under orders of G.O.C., 19th Division. After extremely heavy and sanguinary fighting our troops did all that was required of them, but at a very heavy cost. It was the general opinion of all concerned that never before had there been such destruction and heavy shelling on the part of the enemy. Probably, owing to the exigencies of the services, the R.A.P's taken over from the 41st Division were selected too far back and were all under very heavy shell fire. Their position entailed a great strain on the Regimental bearers and rendered the collection of wounded forward very difficult. The clearing of the R.A.P's was a work which required the utmost devotion to duty, and great credit reflected on the bearers in the way in which they came through. The evacuation from these R.A.P's back almost to the A.D.S. was carried out under the most trying conditions. Forward a perfect hurricane of shells fell and it was there we lost three gallant officers. First, Capt. H. D. Field, O.C. Bearers, received wounds to which he subsequently succumbed. Immediately afterwards Capt. J. H. C. Gatchell, M.O. in charge 11th Royal Sussex, was killed, then another bearer officer, Capt. K. T. Limbery, made the supreme sacrifice. Another bearer officer, Capt. F. W. Stone, fell severely wounded. Notwithstanding these losses the evacuation continued; other officers stepped into the breach and the work was maintained. Officers and men were imbued with the spirit that knew no defeat.

It should be noted that 300 attached Infantry assisted the R.A.M.C. bearers, and did excellent and gallant work. Many casualties occurred in their ranks.

The casualties on this occasion as far as the medical services of the Division were concerned, in addition to those noted above were:

    Killed: O.R's, 9.
    Wounded: Lieut. G. R. Harris.
             Capt. H. F. Warwick at duty.
             Lieut. C. Visger.
             61 O.R's, including five who subsequently died and 9 who remained at duty.

September 27th came as a welcome relief to the Division when it was relieved in the line by the 37th Division and transferred to the IX Corps. In consequence of this and on this day the 134th Field Ambulance handed over its various posts to the 49th Field Ambulance and travelled to Mont Kokerelle Farm in 'buses, taking over a Field Ambulance site from the Ambulance which had relieved it in the line.

One of the first duties to be performed after the Ambulance had settled into its new quarters was to lay to rest the bodies of Capt. Limbery and Corp. Tallon, D.C.M., who also had paid the great price, in the little cemetery of Godeswaervelde. Parties of the various Ambulances attended this sad occasion and thus paid their last respects to these gallant men, leaving them under the serried rows of little wooden crosses and the mud of the newly-dug graves. Pathetic in the rawness of their resting place, and the simplicity of their burial. While the wind made lament through the trees and the rain beat impetuously on a thousand sorrows.

For the month under review the O.C., 134th Field Ambulance recorded in the War Diary, " This has been the hardest month the unit has experienced since its arrival in France. Previous to the two battles it has held the front line for a month with its Bearer Divisions working forward. Its work during operations, assisted by the other Field Ambulances, reflects great credit on all who were engaged. Every individual did his best with the result, that the evacuation was a success and received the congratulations of higher authorities."

October 1st saw the 132nd Field Ambulance move to Keersebrom Camp, Bailleul, having handed over the D.R.S. at Meteren to the 23rd Field Ambulance. After a fortnight here this Ambulance took over the system of evacuation and moved its Headquarters to the A.D.S. at Voormezeele. This A.D.S. was taken over from the 49th Field Ambulance. An A.D.S. at Larch Wood was also occupied by this unit. October 16th saw our Division return to the line, from which it had never really been absent, as four Battalions had been working in the Forward Area, and took over the Tower Hamlet Sector in preparation for the 7th Division's attack, relieving the 37th Division. It was now transferred to X Corps.

The evacuation of this part of the line was as follows: The left R.A.P. was in a small Pill Box. Cases were carried by hand carriage via Relay Post to Canada Street and from right R.A.P. also to Canada Street direct over a trench-board track which was good most of the way except between the left R.A.P. and Relay Post, Bodmin Copse, where the carrying was difficult. The support R.A.P. was located at the Relay Post, this post being a Pill Box also. The right R.A.P. was constructed of an elephant inside a concrete Pill Box forming a roomy and effective shelter. From Canada Street to Larch Wood cases were brought by trolley line or hand carriage, if the line was broken by shelling. This was more often the case than not, although a repair party was constantly at work repairing the damage. From Larch Wood cases were carried to Verbranden Post from whence they were removed by cars to Voormezeele. Here also were the famous Canada Tunnels which had been excavated in the side of a hill and ended in a small chamber some 12 feet square. The smell of which can be long remembered by those who sojourned there.

The stay here, however, was not of long duration as the 7th Division Field Ambulances relieved the posts on the 24th, that Division having relieved our own in the line at this time, and the 132nd Field Ambulance proceeded to X Corps entraining centre at Dickebusche. The 29th, however, saw the Ambulance back again at Voormezeele, our Division having in turn relieved the 7th Division on the night 28/29th October. Capt. Morris of the 132nd Field Ambulance was evacuated, gassed, on the 30th of this month.

As far as the 133rd Field Ambulance was concerned the month of October saw this unit moved to Mont Noir on the 1st, Chippewa Camp having been handed over to the 22nd Field Ambulance. This was a somewhat isolated and unfriendly place on the spur of hills which have already been mentioned. In an adjacent little cemetery was the grave of Major Willie Redmond. Work here proceeded in the erection of tents and marquees, etc., and making them bombproof as far as possible by means of revetments. Whilst here a welcome visit was paid by the Divisional Concert Party, known as the Tivolies. Not long, however, did the Ambulance rusticate, as a move was made on the 12th to a Dysentery Camp at Haegdoorne near Bailleul. At least one man retains vivid memories of the brief stay at Bailleul and the sleeping quarters there. He writes of fossilised holes made by ancient hens and the difficulty of accommodating one's hips to the holes. He also asserts it was here that Capt. G. D. Robertson taught the men scientific louse hunting. Whilst at this place mild excitement was caused by a motor cycle having been stolen from the Cabstand on the night of the 14/15th, followed by the inevitable Court of Enquiry as to why, how and when? The 27th saw a bearer party proceed to A.D.S. Larch Wood and on the 29th Capt. H. K. Stokes was evacuated, gassed.

October was a mild month for the 134th for on the 16th they handed over Mont Kokereele Farm to the 49th Field Ambulance and proceeded to take over Keersebrom from the 132nd Field Ambulance. Whilst this in turn was handed over to the 48th Field Ambulance on the 18th and the unit again moved to the peaceful pastures of Meteren.

Towards the end of the month news was received that the following awards for gallantry had been made:—

132nd Field Ambulance. M.M. to:

    65893   Sergt. R. Dinsdale.
    69659   Private H. T. Francis.
    65867   Private H. Everall.
    72773   Private D. Hartwell.

133rd Field Ambulance. M.M. to:

    77444   Private F. Hodgson.
    72003   Private F. Hodson.
    93945   Sergt. P. J. Mitchelson.
    72169   Private W. C. Daniels.

134th Field Ambulance.   M.M. to:
   M2/147814   Private R. L. Craigs, M.T.
           attached 134th Field Ambulance.

The following Special Order was received from the Army Commander at this time:—

" SPECIAL ORDER

By General Sir H. de la P. Gough, K.C.B., K.C.V.O., Commanding Fifth Army.   30th October, 1917.

Medical Services.

The Army Commander desires to express his appreciation of the excellent work that has been, and is still being done, by the Medical Service in connection with the active operations on this Front. He considers that the manner in which this work has been performed reflects the greatest credit on all concerned.

The evacuation of sick and wounded from the Front to the Casualty Clearing Stations has been most carefully organised and successfully carried out, while the professional skill and attention displayed at the Casualty Clearing Stations, together with increased comfort provided for the patients, has led to highly satisfactory results being obtained.

          H. N. Sargent,   Maj.-Gen.,
      D.A. and Q.M.G., Fifth Army."

The casualties sustained by our Division in this Battle of Menin Road from 31/7/17 to 5/8/17 and from 20/9/17 to 28/9/17 were 204 officers and 6,301 O.R's.

Leave had commenced in the summer of 1917 and towards autumn was in full swing. The witchery and charm of this was above description. Those little pieces of paper that seemed to open the channel ports to one's willing progress were beyond price and value and came to one with the welcome of a legacy or a winning sweep ticket.

Then proceeded the leave-taker to the nearest railhead, it may be Poperinghe, there to wait some hours in a long and jocular train. Unfortunately more than once that leave train at Pop. was hit by enemy shells, with the result that men were transferred to hospital or cemetery and the leave indefinitely postponed. The train, however, set in motion, a slow and tedious journey was made to Boulogne. Here accommodation was provided in one of the famous rest billets, as for instance, Coppings, and many will remember the tremendous scramble which ensued as soon as the canteen opened. Tea, hard-boiled eggs, and such sandwiches as were provided, regaled the happy leave man. Three planks, two short trestles and a couple of filthy blankets, served as means for rest and refreshment. How hot the place could be in summer and how bitter in winter!

Morning saw, breakfast or no breakfast, as the case might be, a long crocodile of rank and file proceeding to the boats. One held one's breath lest they should fill up before one's own turn came, or lest the scrutineers should pounce on one for contraband or illicit souvenirs. But once on board and lifebelts dished out, the great ambition was the first sight of the cliffs of old England. Victoria, with its happy buzz and bustle, was the centre of the world.

The return journey was somewhat different and far less romantic. Laggard feet, and heavy hearts, took us back to Victoria. The cheery greetings were turned to sad farewells. No fascination lay about that sea trip. Whilst the rest camp at St. Martin's, high up amid the wireless masts, was either bleak and dreary or hot and arid. Yet it held attraction for many in the Crown and Anchor boards that lined its entrances and exits.

Then, too, we were hauled up at 1 ack-emma for breakfast, fed with as little ceremony as possible and marched down to draughty trains en route for our respective locations. Who can forget the hours spent at this place on say, a biting cold night in winter. The sheet of ice that covered the top of the hill, the veritable slide down to the station and perhaps a carriage, the door of which would not close! But the leave was worth it and much more, and sufficed for many days to cheer the duckboard tracks and the vermin-infested dug-outs.

November saw two changes as far as our Division was concerned. On the night of 11/12th November the 39th Division relieved the 5th Division and extended its left as far as the Reutelbeek in the Polderhoek Sector and was transferred to IX Corps. Whilst on the 27th our Division was relieved by the 30th Division in the Tower Hamlets and Polderhoek Sectors and transferred to VIII Corps. In the early days of the month news was received by the 132nd Field Ambulance that a Bar to the M.C. had been awarded to Capt. W. T. Brown for gallantry during the operations 19/28th September. And on the 11th this unit became responsible for the evacuation of the line, taking over Woodcote House on the left of the Menin Road, from the 14th Field Ambulance. It was also responsible for Tower Relay Post, Zillebeke, Canada Street, Bodmin Copse, Clapham Junction and the Ecole, Ypres. On the 15th one O.R. was killed and two were wounded of this Ambulance. A Collecting Post was established at Steenvoorde on the 26th and on the 28th the unit moved to Watou, taking over a Field Ambulance site.

The 133rd Field Ambulance having handed over Hagerdoorn Camp to the 50th Field Ambulance on November 2nd, proceeded to renew its acquaintance with Chippewa, taking over from the 21st Field Ambulance. November 5th saw Capt. Harman M.O. in charge 6th Cheshire, evacuated, gassed, and Capt. Ferguson of this unit sent in relief. On November 15th, a holding party was left at Chippewa whilst the main body moved to La Clytte and the schools at Westoutre were taken over from the 2nd New Zealand Field Ambulance. Private G. W. Balcombe of this unit died of wounds on November 20th, which had been received the day before. November 26th saw the unit hand over to the 98th Field Ambulance and proceed to Ouderzeele, taking over from the 96th Field Ambulance. The D.C.M. was conferred upon S/Sergt. 39169 C. T. Williams during the month.

As far as the 134th Field Ambulance was concerned Lieut.-Col. Hildreth vacated command of this unit on November 5th, having received another appointment and on the 9th, Lieut.-Col. C. M. Drew assumed command in his stead. On

November 17th leaving a holding party at Meteren, the unit proceeded to take over a site from the 50th Field Ambulance as a D.R.S. at 8 Rue Benoit Cortyl, Bailleul. On November 25th, this was handed over to the 96th Field Ambulance and a new site for a D.R.S. was occupied by C-section at Hilhoek. The end of the month brought this Ambulance again in contact with Ypres and they were responsible for the evacuation of wounded from the Prison and Beggar's Bush. The M.C. was awarded to Capt. J. H. Porter, of this unit, and to Capt. H. O. H. Willis Bund, M.O. in charge 1/1st Cambs., during this month.

December brought welcome relief to the Division when it was removed to the X Corps area at Lumbres. The 132nd Field Ambulance left Watou on December 8th, the unit marching to Godeswaervelde and there entraining for Lottinghem, marching from thence to billets at Viel Moutier. On the 9th they proceeded to Brunembert.

In sympathy the 133rd Field Ambulance handed over Ouderzeele to the 99th Field Ambulance and entrained at Aleele, detraining at Lottinghen pas de Calais, marching to Viel Moutier. From here Capt. H. F. Warwick and a party took over the X Corps Rest Station at Le Val Restant, Bois de Thiemebronne. This Ambulance, however, was not left long in peace for at 3.30 a.m. on the morning of the 16th an urgent message was received for all available medical aid to be sent to Desures to deal with a collision which had taken place between two troop trains. This was answered by the O.C. and Lieut. Boyer. On the same day, an important date in the calendar was passed, when a Football Match and Tug-of-War, events in the Divisional Competition, took place.

Having handed over the D.R.S. at Hilhoek to the 101st Field Ambulance of the 33rd Division, the 134th Field Ambulance proceeded to entrain at Godewaeresvelde for Affrinques Chateau, at Lannoy. In this delightful area, behind and between Calais and Boulogne, with its rolling country, thread-like roads and extensive forests, the Division now spent a welcome and well-earned rest. The clean and wholesome villages, the magnificent hills and ancient chateaux with Napoleonic associations, provided us with a background of pleasant memories. And when it came to parting, with eternal regrets, as the French would express it. Here the second Christmas on active service was spent, the A.D.M.S. visiting at least one Ambulance during the dinner time and giving them one of his characteristic and stirring addresses.

Christmas barely over, however, that lode star of the Western Front, Ypres, called us back again and the very next day saw the three Ambulances packing up and proceeding to leave this beautiful though wintry countryside.

During the night of Christmas an exceedingly heavy fall of snow was experienced, and by the next morning these exposed roads were well-nigh impassable. The 132nd Field Ambulance sent forward one section which experienced great difficulty in making any progress whatsoever. The transport being snowed up and having to be extricated with much labour. On the 28th an advance party was sent from this unit to take over L'Ebbe Farm, now so well-known to us all. The main body left on the 31st, marching to Affrinques Chateau to billet for the night. On the morning of the 1st, this unit entrained at Wizernes, detraining at St. Jean. A bearer party proceeded at once to Duhallow, whilst the remainder joined the advance party at L'Ebbe Farm. An aid post was also established at Poperinghe.

Similar experience befell the 133rd Field Ambulance when their transport moved forward on the 26th. And on the 28th this unit also moved to Affrinques for the night, entraining at Wizernes on the 29th, and detraining at St. Jean. From here they proceeded to a Field Ambulance site at Duhallow, taking over from the 92nd Field Ambulance, whilst Capt. de Brent and a party took over an A.D.S. at St. Julien.

The 134th Field Ambulance also entrained at Wizernes for the old location of Gwalia Farm on the 29th December.

Thus it befell, that as 1917 opened with the 39th Division holding the line in the famous Ypres Salient, so it closed with the Division, changed maybe, but still the same in character, holding on to the area, the cemeteries of which held so many of its dead. The 39th Division relieved the 32nd Division in the line between 28th and 31st December. It was, however, to a new Salient, that we now returned. Ypres, the scarred and tattered city even more spectral in its mantle of snow, was now becoming a back area. It is true that steel helmets were still ordered to be worn here, but its atmosphere was far healthier than heretofore.

Duhallow had ceased to be an A.D.S. and had assumed the dignity of a Field Ambulance site, while Salvation Corner and the Canal Bank area generally, was losing the significance of former days.

January, 1918, saw the Division holding the line, amid severe and wintry weather, with gales supplementing frost and snow. The posts as far as the medical services were concerned were: Left Sector, R.A.P. at Burns House, with Relay Posts at Winchester Farm and Hubner Farm. Right Sector, R.A.P. Pill Box 83, and Relay Posts at Kronprinz, Albatross and Springfield Farm. Names that will evoke memories in the minds of many.

The month proceeded uneventfully owing, of course, to the time of year and the severity of the weather. As far as the 132nd Field Ambulance was concerned the skin hospital at L'Ebbe Farm occupied their attention until relieved on the 22nd by the 92nd Field Ambulance. The unit then proceeded to the Chateau at Herzeele.

On the 1st of the month, and thus making a good start for the New Year, the 133rd Field Ambulance was supplemented by a party from each of the other Ambulances to assist them in various pieces of work which were being carried out in the forward area. On the 7th this unit moved to a new site at Siege Camp, whilst on the 9th work was commenced on a new A.D.S. at St. Julien to be known as Creagh Castle. The name would suggest a little intimate reminiscence on the part of our

A.D.M.S., though we would hope that the structure bore no other resemblance than in nomenclature with his old and early home. The 22nd saw the unit hand over the various posts to the 106th Field Ambulance and march out to School Camp.

The 134th Field Ambulance found a welcome occupation at the beginning of the month in assisting to move the 32nd C.C.S. to Gwalia Farm, which was surely a sign of the times and the advance that had been made. Whilst towards the middle of the month the idea of the cultivation of available sites in order to relieve the food shortage was put in motion. Thenceforward erstwhile bearers and nurses were devoted to the tilling of virgin spaces. The spade and plough taking the place of stretchers and bandages. On the 18th of the month, a tent section under the charge of Capt. C. D. Coyle, proceeded to Proven School, taking over a hospital from the 2/2nd Home Counties Field Ambulance. The 24th saw the Headquarters of the unit hand over to the 90th Field Ambulance and move to Proven also. Mild excitement was caused on January 13th, when the old chateau at Elverdinge caught fire. Evidently the carelessness of occupying troops served to destroy this well-known refuge of so many officers and men.

And now, after the Division had been continuously in the Salient for some fourteen months, it was at last to seek pastures new. Representations had been made by the medical administration officers time and again that this long spell of service in one area was deleterious to the morale of the troops of the Division. In fact, the D.A.D.M.S.,

Major A. E. Knight, was accused by higher command of having written a letter which should never have been penned by an officer of the British Army. In this he declared that if the Division was not soon relieved then it would be necessary to carry it out of the line. However, such a length of service was surely unique amongst the Divisions on the Western Front, and a record, we imagine, that no other would have wished to emulate.

There were, of course, incidents which relieved the monotony of the mud and slush, even of the Salient, as the following will illustrate.

Four men, not very tall, were carrying down an officer of the Sussex Regiment who had been wounded in the knee. The way was difficult, the bearers often struggling knee deep in mud and water with incidental falls into shell holes though doing their best to keep the case steady. The patient was somewhat restive at the uncomfortable journey and expressed his annoyance at being hit, by many curses. Presently the party emerged on to the Menin Road, when suddenly a German shell landed some distance from them. The bearers lowered the stretcher in order to change over, when to their amazement the wounded officer suddenly leaped off the stretcher and tore down the road as fast as any motor cycle. Those four stood open-mouthed in astonishment, but their subsequent language is unprintable.

AGAIN THE SOMME; AND THE GREAT RETREAT

THE year 1918 was to be to us as to all units of the British Army a memorable year, perhaps even more so to ourselves than to many others. It was, therefore, with great excitement we received the news, towards the end of January, that we were to be removed entirely away from the famous Salient. However, the time worn theory of the "frying pan and the fire" was all too frequently exemplified on the Western Front and in our own case.

In preparation, therefore, for the great trek, the 132nd and the 134th Field Ambulances on the 25th, and the 133rd Field Ambulance on the 26th, entrained at Proven, arriving the next day at Mericourt L'Abbe where they detrained. From here the 132nd Field Ambulance marched to Bray sur Somme where a hospital was opened at the Hospice, while the 133rd marched to Sailley Le Sec, and the 134th Field Ambulance proceeded to a Field Ambulance site at the Chalet, Suzanne. On the 29th, the 132nd Field Ambulance moved to Haut Allaines, the 133rd Field Ambulance also reaching this place the next day. A Main Dressing Station at Fins on the Nurlu Road was taken over from the 27th Field Ambulance of the 9th Division on the 30th, by the 132nd Field Ambulance. Our

Division now took over the Gouzeaucourt Sector of the VII Corps Front, Fifth Army. It should be mentioned here, that owing to the serious wastage of man-power which had taken place it was found necessary to reduce Infantry Brigades from four Battalions to three, which was accomplished in the month of February.

Capt. de Brent, Lieut. Boyer and Lieut. Audus, of the 133rd Field Ambulance with a party proceeded to Nurlu on the 31st, where a D.R.S. was taken over from the 9th South African Field Ambulance. The next day the main body of this unit proceeded to join the advance party at Nurlu. Here considerable work was carried out in the making of this station proof against air raids, as far as that was possible, by means of revetments, constructed about the tents and buildings.

On the 29th the personnel of the 134th Field Ambulance entrained at the Plateau near Mericourt, under Lieut. W. H. Daly, for Heudicourt, where they took over the evacuation of the line. Two A.D.S's, one at Revelon Farm and the other at Queen's Cross were taken over from the 65th Field Ambulance. The Catacombs at Heudicourt were also occupied, which if for no other purpose were useful in the event of the frequent air-raids which were now taking place. For instance, on the night of 30/31st January, the environs of Heudicourt were heavily bombed by enemy aeroplanes.

If Ypres was unfriendly, by reason of the uncharitable actions of the enemy and the exercise of much hate, the area in which we now found ourselves was peculiar in the extreme. A more desolate, stricken and barren land could hardly be imagined. This was the area vacated in great generosity by an obliging foe after the severe fighting of our former battles. A portion of the earth of which the phrase " worth fighting for " seemed an exaggeration. The systematic destruction carried out by the enemy was amazing in its thoroughness. Here again prophetic descriptions were well-nigh powerless. Hardly two bricks on each other, a heap of stones and splintered woodwork marked spots where village elders wielded a calm philosophy, or mayors a variable corporation. German dug-outs were here in abundance and German signs significant in their verbotens. German cemeteries with their crosses simple in their declaration of births and deaths and the suggested sorrow of homefolk. Railway lines, twisted at every joint, declared the pleasure of thorough destruction, while bridges and buildings added to the tale. Churches, utterly gutted, had in many places been turned into cinemas, and notices reminiscent of the sanctity of the place forbade one to spit. In some cases the more important residences had been left, evidently memorials of the various headquarters and the officers of high rank who had slept and bathed within their walls. A large number of tombs in the civilian churchyards had either been broken into by marauders in search of jewels or by shell fire. One broken coffin exposed the long tresses of a dark-haired maiden disturbed even in her last sleep. Truly a land where the bittern might

" boom " with some occasion for his mournful plaint. Peronne and St. Quentin were cities of the plain, visited by a pestilence more certain than that of Sodom and Gomorrah.

We had not been here long, however, before various conferences took place regarding the possibility of certain German activities, for the German plans of their projected advance were well known to our Headquarters long before they actually took place. Full medical arrangements were therefore pushed forward in preparation for defence and, if necessary, evacuation. Reconnaissances were made, sites for medical institutions selected and routes for the various lines of evacuation marked out. It was also arranged that the 132nd Field Ambulance should be responsible for the evacuation of the line when the emergency arose, assisted by personnel and equipment from the other two Field Ambulances and 200 attached infantry bearers and 6 officers. There were talks of red lines, green lines, brown lines and subdued excitement prevailed as to what would happen. A new A.D.S. was projected and commenced building at the Sugar Refinery by the 134th Field Ambulance, while on the 20th February a small raid was carried out by the 11th Royal Sussex, evidently in search of information that would be of use to the Division.

Meanwhile, a Dressing Station was established at Sorel le Grand by the 132nd Field Ambulance who also received orders to run a small Ambulance train from the siding of the Deacauville light railway to the C.C.S. at Tincourt. This train, which consisted of two covered wagons, warmed by oil stoves, each capable of taking 12 stretcher cases, called at the D.R.S., Nurlu, and the 16th Division M.D.S., at Villers Faucon,

About the middle of February Sir Douglas Haig was seen in the Divisional area and paid a visit to Major-Gen. Feetham at D.H.Q., then stationed at Nurlu. A very disastrous incident occurred on the 16th, when a bomb was dropped on the Divisional Canteen at Fins, killing 10 and wounding 15. A second bomb was dropped on a dug-out of the 39th D.A.C., killing 2 and wounding 9. The 132nd Field Ambulance being called upon to deal with these casualties. As far as this unit was concerned preparations were made on the 1st March to deal with an emergency. On the 12th this Ambulance moved to Haut Allaines where a mutual exchange was effected with a South African Field Ambulance.

The 133rd Field Ambulance had a welcome visit paid them by the 39th Divisional Tivolies on the 23rd February, when an excellent evening was provided for both patients and personnel. The next day one of the few and memorable football matches was played by this unit against No. 1 D.A.C. On the 28th one of those little irresolutions was enacted, of which the celebrated Duke of York was considered to have had the monopoly, when the unit marched out of Nurlu at 9 o'clock, the order being countermanded and they promptly returned. On March 6th high festival prevailed in this unit when they enjoyed a famous spread at tea-time in order to celebrate the completion of

two years' service with the Expeditionary Force.
March 11th saw this Ambulance march to Moislains
where they relieved the 28th Field Ambulance.

The Belgian Croix de Guerre was awarded to
46092 Private W. Kirkham of the 134th Field
Ambulance on February 9th, whilst on the 23rd
Sergt. McLean and 6 others, including Privates
Godfrey, Spokes and Westwood of this unit, were
wounded at Relay Post A, near Gouzeaucourt.
Another raid was carried out by the 17th K.R.R.
on the 27th, followed on the 9th March by a still
further raid made by the 11th Royal Sussex in
front of Gouzeaucourt.

The 27th Field Ambulance relieved the 134th
Field Ambulance at Heudecourt on the 11th March
and this unit proceeded to a new site at Gurlu
Wood. To celebrate this event and the change of
air and scenery, a football match was played, which
on the 17th was followed by another versus the
A.S.C., resulting in F.A. 2 and A.S.C. nil.

Meanwhile events were moving with some rapidity
as far as the Division was concerned. Major-Gen.
E. Feetham, the Divisional Commander, was absent
from the Division on leave, his place being taken
by the C.R.A., Brig.-Gen. G. A. S. Cape. The
Division had been relieved in the Gouzeaucourt
Sector by the 9th Division on the 12th March
and had gone into G.H.Q. Reserve under the
VII Corps. Whilst in reserve the 118th Infantry
Brigade carried out training and the 116th and 117th
Infantry Brigades continued work on various lines
in the VII Corps system of defence. The

Field Corps R.E., the pioneer Battalion 13th Glosters, with one Battalion 116th Infantry Brigade, were detached to a considerable distance for similar work under the Fifth Army.

Whilst in Corps Reserve, all officers reconnoitred the green and brown lines and the best routes for counter attacks. Orders for the assembly of the Division in Corps . Reserve were issued and a tactical exercise, without troops, involving a counter attack on Ronssoy was carried out by the Staff and Battalion Commanders of the 116th Infantry Brigade under the direction of Brig.-Gen. Cape. During these exercises a salvo of 77 m.m. shells killed Gen. Cape and severely wounded Capt. L. E. H. Whitby of the M.G. Co., affiliated to 116th Infantry Brigade. Brig.-Gen. M. L. Hornby, C.M.G., D.S.O., now assumed temporary command of the Division. This sad occurrence was on March 18th, and on March 20th, with due military honours, the body of General Cape was buried.

On the night of 20/21st March, units of the 39th Division were located as under:—

D.H.Q. Camp between Haut Allaines and Moislains.

    Divisional Artillery, Peronne (training).

    Divisional Engineers, 1 Field Co., Falvy.
                       1 Field Co., Tincourt.
                       1 Field Co., Templeux la
                       Fosse and Maricourt.

116th Infantry Brigade, H.Q. Gurlu Wood.
    11th Royal Sussex, Hem.
    1 Battalion Hamel.
    1 Battalion, Gurlu Wood.

117th Infantry Brigade, H.Q., Nurlu.
    3 Battalions, Heudecourt-Sorel area.

118th Brigade, Moislains.
    13th Glosters, Beaumetz.
    Divisional M.G. Battalion, Haut Allaines.

The VII Corps Front extended from L'Empire to North of Gouzeacourt and was held by the 16th, 21st and 9th Divisions. At 4.50 a.m. on March 21st, the enemy opened a bombardment on the whole of the Corps Front, but heaviest on that of the Right (16th) Division with gas in the Battery areas.

At 5.15 a.m. orders were received from VII Corps to man Battle Stations and the code word putting into force the orders previously issued was wired to all concerned.

The 132nd Field Ambulance, who had been allocated the work of evacuation when the emergency arose, at once moved to their battle station near Nurlu and parked themselves there. As this position became untenable owing to shell fire they moved back to a Quarry where they took refuge for the time being. From here a bearer sub-division and three horsed ambulances were sent to the assembly point of the 117th Infantry Brigade at Sorel Wood, under Major W. T. Brown, M.C. Later, as the Brigade moved back, the Ambulance moved with them to Saulcourt.

During the morning frequent reports received indicated that the enemy was held on the whole of the Corps Front, except on that of the Right (16th) Division. At mid-day the mist which had been very thick since dawn had practically cleared, though visibility remained very indifferent throughout the day.

The 133rd Field Ambulance now received instructions to clear their hospital, all cases of Scabies having to be returned to their units. There was soon accommodation at Moislains for 600 stretcher cases.

Except for heavy shelling of positions occupied by the 117th Infantry Brigade which necessitated several moves on the part of the Brigade concerned, the Division remained in its concentration area without incident until 2 p.m. in the afternoon, when orders were received for the Divisional Artillery to reinforce the 16th Division, whose position in the battle zone had been turned to the right flank. Accordingly, the two Artillery Brigades moved to positions North of Roisel and about Longavesnes and came under the orders of B.G., R.A., 16th Division.

At 1.45 p.m. VIII Corps issued a wire ordering the 116th Infantry Brigade to be placed at the disposal of the 16th Division. The 11th Royal Sussex, who had already proceeded from Hem by route march were met by motor 'buses and conveyed to Grange Camp, the remaining units, with a Company of the M.G. Battalion attached, moving from Gurlu Woods to assembly positions along the railway running from Villers Faucon to Epehy, assembly being completed by dark.

The 132nd Field Ambulance was in close touch with 117th Infantry Brigade at 2 p.m., but later was ordered to get in touch with a Field Ambulance of the 16th Division, and moved its Headquarters to the old C.C.S. site at Tincourt, establishing itself there by 8.30 a.m. on March 22nd. The O.C. bearers, Major Brown, established his Headquarters at Longavesnes in order to collect wounded from the 118th Brigade who had moved to this vicinity, leaving Major Uloth to evacuate for the 117th Brigade. Later in the day the Ambulance moved to Doignt.

From this hour, until the early morning of the 23rd when it again came under orders of the 39th Division, no very definite information was forthcoming as to the rôle played by the 116th Infantry Brigade. It was, however, heavily engaged on the morning of the 22nd, taking part in the recapture of St. Emilie where the 1st Battalion of the Herts. Regiment displayed marked gallantry. The wounded were, of course, evacuated under arrangements of the 16th Division, R.A.M.C.

At 4 p.m., orders were received for the 118th Brigade and at 5 p.m. for the 117th Brigade, each with one Machine Gun Co. to dig, occupy and wire a switch line from the Brown Line at Saulcourt to the Green Line at Tincourt Wood. Lieut.-Col. Couchman (C.R.E.), Lieut.-Col. Burland (G.S.O.2) and Capt. Carr (G.S.O.3), were at once ordered to proceed to 21st Divisional Headquarters North-east of Longavesnes to meet representatives of the 117th and 118th Brigades and to tape out the line. Arrangements were also made to form a dump of the necessary tools and R.E. material by lorry.

The 117th Brigade moved by route march via Lieramont, the 118th Brigade, two Battalions by route march, Brigade Headquarters and one Battalion M.G.Co. by lorries via Templeux la Fosse to dig the left and right sections of the switch respectively.

The last Battalion of the Brigade was guided to its work shortly before midnight, by which time a thick mist had come down, which together with the darkness, considerably hampered operations. Considerable difficulty was experienced in getting the line correctly sited, but by daylight on the 22nd March a very good chain of posts existed with some wire in front, put up by the 227th and half of the 234th Field Corps. R.E., and the 13th Glosters.

At 10.50 p.m. the situation on the VII Corps Front appeared to be as follows: The 16th Division, reinforced by the 116th Infantry Brigade, two Companies of which were in St. Emilie, held the Brown Line from the Corps right flank to North of St. Emilie. Thence the line followed approximately the railway round and East of Epehy, held by the 21st Division, to Railton and thence via Genin Well Copse No. 1; 9th Division, East of Chapel Hill to Chapel Crossing, along the railway to the West of Gauche Wood, through Quentin Redoubt and thence along the original Front Line.

At 12.30 a.m., March 22nd, orders were received from VII Corps to the effect that the 21st Division was to hold Epehy and extend their front to meet the 16th Division about 900 yards North of St. Emilie Station, and that the 39th Division, less 116th Brigade, was to hold Tincourt Wood,

Saulcourt Switch, twelve tanks being placed at their disposal to assist.

Orders to this effect were issued to the units and general instructions given as to the front to be held should a retirement to the Green Line become necessary. As on the 21st a heavy mist prevailed until noon.

Lieut.-Col. F. W. Gossett, C.M.G., D.S.O. (G.S.O.1) left D.H.Q. at 8.30, and visited the switch line where he found all quiet, except for shelling of the two villages, which was not heavy but continuous. The switch line consisted of a series of platoon posts with some wire in front, and occasional trenches for supporting platoons, one per company in reserve.

117th Brigade Headquarters were found to be established in the old Headquarters of the 21st Division together with the Headquarters of the Right Brigade of the latter Division.

At 8.45 a.m., VII Corps telephoned G.S.O.2 that the Germans were pushing in on the right of the Right Division and that arrangements were to be made to fall back to the Green Line if required.

At 9.15 a.m. the 116th Infantry Brigade reported that the enemy had broken into St. Emilie, but there was no threat against the front held by the 117th and 118th Brigades.

At 10 o'clock a.m., VII Corps Headquarters closed at Templeux la Fosse and reopened at Clery, 29th D.H.Q. going to Templeux and the 16th Division to Doingt, rear Headquarters.

At 3.10 p.m., the 117th Brigade reported that the Germans were advancing slowly on the line Capron Copse—Villers Faucon and the switch line.

Meanwhile the 133rd Field Ambulance at Moislains had been visited by enemy aircraft on the night of the 21/22nd and a large number of casualties amongst patients and personnel had resulted. Amongst those killed was Private Hills. The bombing would have resulted in considerably more casualties but for the fact that most of the patients had been cleared out previously, 400 walking cases having been sent under the charge of the Senior Chaplain, C. of E., Rev. J. Crawley, to Maricourt. This unit had passed through over 1,000 cases, doing excellent work. They moved from here to Combles, marching out at 11.30 on the 22nd.

The 134th Field Ambulance had remained parked at Gurlu Wood on the 21st, but from 10 a.m. onwards came well within the zone of shelling. They were busily engaged all the morning in dressing and evacuating wounded, sending them back as well as possible to the 133rd Field Ambulance at Moislains. This unit also established a forward dump of clothing and made arrangements for dealing with slightly gassed cases. In addition to the 132nd Field Ambulance they also maintained liason with the two Brigades. They moved to St. Denis Corner on the Nurlu-Peronne Road, proceeding from here later in the day to Haut Allaines, parking on the Clery Road, where they spent the night in the open.

A most remarkable sight was now witnessed behind our lines. The roads, stretching as they did like ribbons amongst the open rolling country, were literally black with moving traffic, traffic moving in one direction only, viz., Westwards. Every conceivable kind of formation was encamped by the roadside. Tanks moved slowly into concentration areas, finally to be abandoned owing to shortage of petrol. Guns which had been firing in one direction in the morning were directing their fire to enfilading positions in the afternoon, before being limbered up and dragged out to other positions. Towards evening fires were seen in many places as the various stores and camps were destroyed prior to evacuation. And with it all there was a note of cheerfulness amongst the Other Ranks that was not reflected in the Higher Command. Perhaps it was the sense of movement, a pleasant experience after months of stagnation, certainly it was the outcome of new scenes and the novelty of the situation.

Orders had now been received from VII Corps that the Army policy was to fight a rearguard action and delay the enemy. The 39th Division was ordered to hold the switch line with one Brigade and the Green Line from Tincourt Wood to the railway south of Hamel with the other. Two other lines were manned further back known as the Corps Line and the Maisonette Line, in case of necessity.

At 2.45 p.m., after a telephone conversation with the 21st Division, the 117th Infantry Brigade was ordered to conform to any retirement of the latter from Saulcourt.

At 3.50 p.m., the 117th Infantry Brigade reported that the Tincourt Wood, Saulcourt Switch, was heavily attacked and that a defensive flank was being organised from North-west of Guillemont Copse towards Lieramont.

At 6 p.m., instructions from VII Corps ordered a withdrawal to the Green Line on the whole Corps Front. This was followed by instructions at 6.15 p.m. to hold the retirement in abeyance and that the Southern flank of the Corps would be North of Bouchy.

At 8 p.m., orders were received for the withdrawal as previously ordered to take place and in consequence the withdrawal from the portion of the Switch Line still held and from the defensive flanks, commenced at 9.30 p.m. in conjunction with the withdrawal of the 21st Division. This was effected in good order. Between 8.30 p.m. on March 22nd and 2 a.m. on the 23rd, Lieut.-Col. Burland, G.S.O.2, visited the whole front held by the 39th Division and found the Brigades holding the Green Line.

By nightfall therefore on the second day of the German attack we were in the last of our defensive positions, which were only to be occupied after days of fighting and as a last resource.

At 7.30 p.m., 39th Divisional Artillery and 282nd and 150th Army Brigades R.F.A. were placed under the orders of our Division. During the 22nd the 39th Division had been heavily engaged.

The Divisional Artillery was ordered at 9 a.m., March 22nd, to withdraw to their Green Line positions. The 186th Brigade R.F.A. with limbers close to their guns remained in action up to the last possible moment. In the case of some guns the enemy were within 300 yards when the withdrawal took place. In the case of the 174th Brigade only D Battery had its limbers up in time and got away.

The remaining Batteries continued to fire at such targets as were available in the prevailing low visibility, after our own infantry had retired behind them, and when the detachments were finally withdrawn by order of the Battery Commanders, taking with them all breech blocks and sights. They were actually under machine gun fire from the rear as well as the flanks of their positions.

D Battery, 174th Brigade, occupied an intermediate position 500 yards North of Tincourt until 8 p.m., doing good work in dispersing enemy troops and transports assembling North of Marquaix.

At 5 a.m., March 23rd, a medical officer was sent forward to 117th B.H.Q. from the 132nd Field Ambulance with a bearer division to assist the other bearers. The second bearer division worked through Drincourt and Bussu, and as the situation developed these bearers cleared wounded between Bussu and Peronne, falling back in touch with our retiring troops.

At 12.15 a.m., the 116th Infantry Brigade again came under the orders of the 39th Division, and at 6.15 p.m. the retirement to the Corps Line which had been reconnoitred by the C.R.E. and worked on by the Divisional R.E. on the 22nd was ordered to commence at 8 a.m.

The 116th Infantry Brigade was ordered to occupy the Corps Line by 6 a.m. The 117th Brigade withdrew through the left and the 118th Brigade through the right of the 116th Brigade.

At 8 a.m., Major-Gen. E. Feetham, C.B., C.M.G., returned from leave and took over command of the Division from Brig.-Gen. M. L. Hornby who reassumed command of the 116th Brigade.

The enemy was pressing his attacks with great vigour and any withdrawal was followed up by strong bodies of troops and Field Artillery. Owing to the situation further South it was clear that a further withdrawal would have to take place and at 9.40 a.m. three Field Companies were ordered to move back and prepare a line running from La Maisonnette to Biaches.

At 9 a.m. Doignt was evacuated by the 132nd Field Ambulance and during the operations in front of this place and rearwards, motor ambulances were sent up to the nearest possible point to assist in the removal of the wounded. Evacuation at this time was most difficult and reflected great credit on all ranks in their devotion to duty. It should be noted that the 132nd Field Ambulance was the last unit to leave Doignt and did so only when our troops were retiring before the enemy over the adjacent crest. The retirement was carried out in good order, through Peronne and across the river. About two hours later, the bearer officers and bearers rejoined Headquarters, having cleared all the wounded which they had collected. The work of these officers and men was deserving of great praise. They maintained touch with the infantry and practically came through the gap in their Company, bringing the wounded with them in spite of all enemy devices to render their work futile. There were many casualties at this stage from aircraft machine gun fire.

At 6.30 p.m., this Ambulance was in position behind the 118th Infantry Brigade, 1,000 yards from the front line. Orders were issued for a withdrawal and the main body of the unit moved back. O.C. bearers remained at B.H.Q. to act as bearer officers and control the forward situation with bearers and motors. This evacuation proved very satisfactory as it enabled the clearing of the wounded of the 117th Brigade to Feuilleres, in addition to direct clearing of the 118th Brigade.

Throughout the day both during the withdrawal from the Corps Line to the St. Denis Line and subsequently to La Maisonette—Biaches Line, the roads running West, through Peronne and Clery, were heavily congested with all manner of traffic, In every case the enemy was held long enough to enable the traffic to get clear.

Fortunately, the enemy made but little use of his aircraft in harrassing this congestion of impedimenta, had he done so the confusion must have been very terrible and our position made much worse than it actually was.

Early on the 23rd the 134th Field Ambulance was ordered to Clery and about 1 p.m., as the situation developed, it was ordered to a point between Feuilleres and Herbecourt, accompanied by its

own transport and that of the 132nd Field
Ambulance. At 10 o'clock that night it was
considered advisable to move again, and it accordingly proceeded to a site on the Herbecourt-Cappy
Road.

Also on this day the 133rd Field Ambulance was
ordered to evacuate Combles, cross the river and
proceed to Flaucourt, whilst later in the day the
unit again moved, proceeding to Cappy, which
it reached in the early hours of the morning of the
24th. Here a great discovery was made in the Corps
Rest Station that had been hurriedly evacuated.
The 133rd Field Ambulance was not slow to
take possession. A Dressing Station was established
on this site and about 200 wounded evacuated.
Higher authorities were informed and much of the
valuable stores were salved. To say nothing of the
pleasant harvest of food that was willingly disposed
of by the hungry personnel.

To return, however, to the chronicle of events
of the Division, the 282nd A.F.A. Brigade, which
were temporarily attached to the 39th Division,
was caught in the act of limbering up to withdraw
from their position about Mt. St. Quentin and
only got away with six of its guns.

At 1 p.m., orders were issued to Infantry Brigades
to prepare to withdraw to the Maisonette—Biaches
Line and at 4.15 p.m., the 118th Brigade moved
back to join the three Field Companies in the
preparation of the new line. The 116th Brigade
and the 13th Glosters, who were now acting as a
fighting unit, and the 117th Brigade, followed shortly
afterwards covering their withdrawal by rear guards.

The river was crossed at Halle and Clery and the retirement successfully effected, though the crossing was considerably harrassed by machine gun fire from hostile aeroplanes and constant shell fire. During these operations Brig.-Gen. M. L. Hornby, commanding 116th Brigade was severely wounded. In the afternoon the G.O.C. accompanied by G.S.O.2 visited the new line.

By nightfall on March 23rd, the 39th Division was holding a line running from La Maisonette, along the line of the Canal to a point immediately South of Ommiecourt-les-Clery, a position of considerable strength as all bridges across the river, with the exception of one, which was dealt with later, had been demolished by the R.E.

D.H.Q. left Clery during the afternoon and were established in a house at Frise.

The 66th Division was now on the right of the 39th Division, and touch was successfully established with them in the new line. It was, however, found necessary to move the 116th Infantry Brigade to the North of the Somme to maintain touch with the 21st Division. A move that was successfully carried out during the night. The 117th Brigade having been withdrawn to Feuilleres, the defence of the forward zone remained with the 118th Infantry Brigade.

The 16th Division, which up to this time had been fighting on the Division's right, had been practically squeezed out of the line, and during the night orders were received for the relief of the remnants of this Division by the 118th Brigade. The 16th Division was withdrawn into Corps Reserve at Cappy.

The night of the 23/24th March passed quietly and every effort was made to reorganise units. This proved to be a matter of great difficulty as stragglers of several Divisions were now mingled with the ranks of our own. Platoon organisation had temporarily ceased to exist. The crossing of the Somme had also led to confusion among units and several elements of the 39th Division—two Companies of the 4/5th Black Watch—had been discovered in the ranks of the 21st Division—got separated from their units and retired through Clery-sur-Somme, North of the river.

The enemy troops in Peronne appeared to be in high spirits and loud singing could be heard by our men on the right.

During the morning the G.O.C. made a reconnaissance of the whole front line and visited all Brigade Headquarters. On returning to D.H.Q. he expressed himself fully satisfied with this position, though there were a large number of stragglers on the road of many Divisions.

With so strong an obstacle as the Somme in front of our troops it was expected that the enemy would be successfully held for some days.

At 6 a.m., March 24th, the 132nd Field Ambulance again moved and established an Advanced Collecting Post at Herbecourt. It is interesting to note that the Headquarters of this Ambulance at this time was under direct observation of the enemy. Notwithstanding this, the site was maintained until midnight of the 25th. In the afternoon of this day all transport other than horsed ambulances, water carts and one limber, was ordered back to the 134th Field Ambulance.

In conversation with the Corps Commander at this time the G.O.C. expressed his confidence in the ability of the Division to maintain its present position without difficulty and without the assistance of the 1st Cavalry Division, which was at this time at the disposal of the VII Corps and whose Headquarters were expected to arrive at Frise.

Throughout the morning of the 24th strong enemy forces were seen pushing forward between Clery and Rancourt, where they were harrassed by the fire of our artillery and machine guns in enfilade. Particularly was this the case in the roads, where our artillery caused much havoc and confusion. One detached section with an attached Battery R.H.A. took up various positions facing North on the ridge North-east of Herbecourt and did extremely good work over open sights. Many excellent targets for our artillery were, however, missed owing to difficulty of liason between the artillery and infantry. A difficulty which existed throughout the retreat and which proved to be one of the greatest problems of the operations.

At 3 p.m., the 16th Divisional Artillery Group, consisting of the 180th Brigade R.F.A., 227th Army Brigade R.F.A., and elements of the 174th and 189th Brigades R.F.A., came under orders of the C.R.A., 39th Division. During the day the average number of rounds fired per battery was 3,000, most of which was observed fire.

During the afternoon telephone messages were received from Corps to say that the enemy was forcing the passage of the Somme at Brie Pagny and Bethencourt and that the Northern flank of this Corps was being turned by strong enemy forces in the neighbourhood of Saillisel. Owing to this factor arising it was intimated that a further withdrawal must be contemplated and that the VII Corps would take up a line running from Frise to the junction with the XIX Corps. Accordingly the Field Companies R.E. commenced work on a line running from Becquincourt to Frise. The enemy movements North of the Somme continued until dark.

Owing to the situation it was found necessary to move the 134th Field Ambulance to a site between Bray and Cappy on the 24th.

The evening was remarkable for a series of wild rumours that got abroad. This was probably the work of enemy agents whose activities were expected to be great. It was constantly reported that the enemy had crossed the river at Biaches, a report which, though the bridge there had not been completely destroyed, was without foundation. It was also rumoured that the enemy was advancing through Barieux and Estrees on Cappy, which rumour was confirmed by an order issued by the 16th Division, apparently without any reference to higher authority.

At this time, as our Division was out of touch with the Corps owing to the line being down, and as we should have been placed in an extremely precarious position in the event of any such advance by the enemy, the G.S.O.1 motored to Corps Headquarters to find out the situation. His temporary absence prevented the G.O.C. from attending the Corps Commanders' Conference at Maricourt. The G.S.O.1 returned to say that all the rumours were without foundation. A despatch rider also returned from Estrees with the information that the Headquarters of the 66th Division were still established there.

The Division on our left North of the Somme had now been forced back on to a line Curlu—Maurepas, which left our flank exposed. The 117th Infantry Brigade was ordered to hold the line of the Canal from Buscourt to Feuilleres and later to extend their left to Frise. Touch was to be established here with the 16th Division who had moved from Cappy to secure the crossing over the river Westward.

The R.E. demolished the bridge at Feuilleres and succeeded in completing the demolition of the Halle bridge at 10 p.m. The Frise bridge was blown up at 1 a.m. on the 25th.

At 1 a.m. D.H.Q. moved from Frise to Chuignes. By this time, owing to casualties and disorganisation among formations, Infantry Brigades could not be relied upon to provide formed bodies of more than average strength of 20 officers and 600 O.R.'s per Brigade.

At 4.30 a.m. the Division came under the orders of the XIX Corps, the boundary line between the VII and XIX Corps being the River Somme. The 116th Infantry Brigade who had been

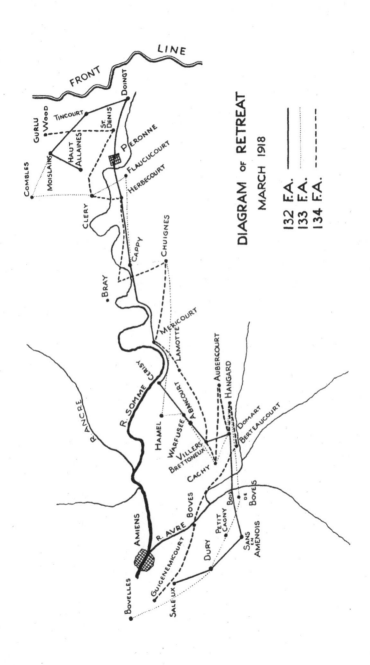

DIAGRAM of RETREAT
MARCH 1918

132 F.A. ——————
133 F.A. ················
134 F.A. — — — —

FRONT LINE

GURLU WOOD
COMBLES
TINCOURT
MOISLAINS
HAUT ALLAINES
ST. DENIS
DOINGT
PERONNE
FLAUCUCOURT
HERBECOURT
CLERY
CHUIGNES
CAPPY
BRAY
MERICOURT
LAMOTTE
AUBERCOURT
HANGARD
R. SOMME CRISY
HAMEL
WARFUSEE
ABANCOURT
VILLERS BRETTONEUX
DOMART
BERTEAUCOURT
CACHY
RANCRE
BOIS
DE
BOVES
AMIENS
R. AVRE
BOVES
PETIT CAGNY
SANS AMENOIS
GUIGENEMICOURT
BOVELLES
DURY
SALEUX

extricated from the fight by the 21st Division and concentrated in the Suzanne area, was ordered to cross the Somme and assemble at Chuignolles, where they would be in Divisional Reserve.

At 4.15 p.m., orders were received from Corps for the Division to withdraw to the line Herbecourt—Frise, both inclusive, which was necessary owing to the enemy's continued advance further South, about Flaucourt and Assevillers. As withdrawal was to commence at dark, little time was available for the construction of any defences, but some R.E. labour was made use of before the Infantry Brigade fell back. In sympathy with this the 134th Field Ambulance was now moved to near Chuignes and at midnight it was finally moved to Mericourt sur Somme.

Before dark, small bodies of the enemy had already succeeded in crossing the river and reaching La Maisonette Ridge. A counter attack organised by the G.O.C. 118th Brigade unfortunately did not materialise owing to the unit delegated to carry it out, viz., 1/6th Cheshires, having been given orders by a General of the 66th Division of which G.O.C., 118th Brigade, was not informed.

During the withdrawal the Cambridgeshires were somewhat heavily attacked in Biaches, but delayed the enemy long enough to prevent our troops being much harrassed. The night in the new line passed quietly.

Owing to the development of the situation, the Headquarters of the 132nd Field Ambulance was ordered back to Cappy at midnight on the 25th and during the night the Advanced Collecting Post was moved to Dompierre and later fell back to Chuignes. The 133rd Field Ambulance relinquished the pleasant position of Cappy to the 132nd Field Ambulance and marched to Chuignolles, spending the night of the 25th there. The next day they proceeded to Hamel.

On the early morning of the 26th the Corps telephoned to say that it was possible a further withdrawal to a line Rouvroy—Proyart would be necessary. Accordingly the Engineers were assembled at Cappy and proceeded to dig a line of posts running in front of Proyart and Framerville. At 7 a.m. the enemy heavily attacked our line about Herbecourt and turned the flank of the 118th Infantry Brigade on the right forcing them to fall back, to which movement our left Brigade, the 117th, were compelled to conform. The 116th Brigade was moved up from Chuignolles to cover the withdrawal and operate on the right of the 118th Brigade. B.H.Q. of 116th and 118th Brigades were now established at Chuignes and D.H.Q. moved to Proyart.

On the morning of the 26th instructions were issued to 132nd Field Ambulance to move back from Cappy to Mericourt sur Somme. This withdrawal was carried out rapidly as the unit was not hampered with transport. All wounded were cleared before evacuating the hospital at Cappy by the courageous use of motor ambulances. The M.T. drivers carried out their work in a manner deserving of great praise.

This ambulance had, therefore, been continuously working the line, behind troops fighting a rearguard action and against overwhelming odds. Sleep or rest was practically out of the question and it is to their great credit, from the O.C. to the latest joined reinforcement, that all the work was carried out in a manner worthy of the highest traditions of the Corps. Time after time the forward bearers of this unit were side by side with the front line troops. These remarks of course apply also to the bearers of the 134th Field Ambulance who were attached to the 132nd Field Ambulance at this time.

It was now decided to relieve the 132nd Field Ambulance in the evacuation of the line on their arrival at Mericourt sur Somme, and accordingly the 134th Field Ambulance was ordered to take over the work. The 132nd Field Ambulance on relief was ordered to concentrate at Ceresy and on completion to move to Warfusee—Abancourt where they were billeted for the night in an empty farm. All spare transport of the Divisional Ambulance was here attached to them.

In spite of continuous marching the 134th Field Ambulance now assumed responsibility for the evacuation of the line, taking over at 11 a.m. on the morning of the 26th in the finest spirits. The Headquarters of this unit was now moved behind the Proyart Line and a Main Dressing Station was opened at La Motte, the forward officer being in touch with Brigade. From now onwards, owing to the rapidly developing situation, many wounded came in and frequent withdrawals were necessary, the first being to Villers Brettoneux with an A.D.S. at La Motte.

Orders were now received for the withdrawal of the Division to the Framerville—Proyart Line, both villages exclusive to our Division. It was to be conducted as slowly as possible so that the new line would not be occupied until dusk. At the commencement the right flank of the 118th Brigade was found to be in the air owing to a somewhat precipitate retirement of the 66th Division. Patrols were therefore sent out to obtain touch with the 50th Division, the next farthest South, which was effected after great difficulty and necessitated a considerable extension of front.

It was found impossible to hold the enemy long enough to allow of occupation of the new line at dark, and Brigades reported they were in position as early as 4.30 in the afternoon. To secure the line until Brigades had completed occupation, the R.E., who had been carrying out the work, were ordered to man the posts, and the Signal School was ordered up from Hamel with instructions to withdraw as soon as the Infantry Brigades were established in the line.

The 16th Division had previously moved troops through Proyart to continue the line from the village to the Somme.

The withdrawal of the Artillery was carried out by batteries without loss, and new positions were taken up in the Morcourt Valley. D.H.Q. moved back from Proyart to Hamel at 3 p.m. and the three B.H.Q. established themselves in a large farm North of La Motte-Foucaucourt Road. The line was held by the 117th Infantry Brigade on the left and the 118th Infantry Brigade on the right. The troops holding the village were unfortunately driven through Framerville before the enemy's advance was held, and a local counter attack failed to retake it, though it succeeded in driving the enemy back some 200 yards.

116th Infantry Brigade was assembled about a mile in rear of the centre of our line as Divisional Reserve and placed at the disposal of Brig.-Gen. Armytage. Field Corps were withdrawn to Morcourt as also the 13th Glosters, the latter after once being ordered back into the line by a Brigadier of another Division ready to assist 16th Division to stop any attempt to cross the river or to form a defensive flank should the 16th Division be driven back. The night passed without incident on the Divisional front, though information was received that the enemy held the North bank of the Somme as far West as Chipilly. The Division on our left reported being heavily attacked during the night along the Somme Valley, and the number of stragglers of all Divisions on roads behind the front was very large. At dawn, March 27th, the enemy launched a faint-hearted attack along the whole of our front, but made no headway. An air reconnaissance revealed that the enemy was bringing up troops in motor 'buses to Chuignes and Fontaine les Cappy. These troops were apparently diverted along the Valley of the Somme, as at 11 a.m. the 16th Division reported the enemy had broken through the centre between Proyart and the Somme.

This compelled the 117th Brigade at 11.30 a.m. to form a defensive flank and the 116th Brigade with the 13th Glosters were ordered to continue the line along the spur S.E. of Morcourt while the 186th Brigade R.F.A. was compelled to withdraw to new positions. In many cases before retiring a considerable amount of execution was done by the artillery over open sights. During the day the 132nd Field Ambulance marched to Warfusee and later proceeded to Cachy.

At 12.15 p.m. the 117th Brigade was compelled to withdraw, the left flank being badly exposed, and, in spite of a counter attack by the 118th Brigade which temporarily succeeded in completely restoring the line on the right.

About 2 p.m., the enemy succeeded in forcing a passage over the Somme at Cherisy, held by 70 men of the 16th Division, and was thus on the left rear of the 39th Division. Meanwhile on the North bank of the Somme, the enemy had succeeded in establishing himself as far West as Sailly-le-Sec, and had commenced to shell Hamel with some consistency. D.H.Q. received a direct hit and moved from here to Hamelet under instructions from Corps. Before settling here, however, orders were received to move to Fouilloy.

A further retirement by the 16th Division about 2.30 p.m., again exposed the flank of the 117th Brigade and a defensive flank, facing North, was formed by the 118th Brigade on high ground half a mile South of Morcourt. Headquarters of the three Brigades were on the main road two and a half miles due East of La Motte en Santerre. Information was received at 12 noon that one Battalion of the D.L.I. and one of the Devons were being sent to the assistance of the Division to counter attack Proyart and at 4 p.m. the attack was launched. This was only partially successful. About 4 p.m. the G.O.C. and G.S.O.1 proceeded via XIX Corps Headquarters and along the main Amiens—Faucoucourt Road and saw both Brigades with a view to ascertaining the exact position. En route the Divisional Commander personally organised the numerous stragglers of our Division, falling back along the main road, and initiated two counter attacks towards the North and North-east which succeeded in establishing positions in the woods and securing several prisoners. The G.O.C. passed through La Motte en Santerre on his return journey about 6.30 p.m. and found it held by men of various units not of the 39th Division.

By about 7.30 p.m. the enemy succeeded in forcing his way into La Motte en Santerre, cutting all direct communication between our Division and its Brigades, which were thus surrounded on three sides.

Orders were now received from XIX Corps that our Division was to hold the line then occupied to the last, and Lieut. Rorke, of the 39th Division Signals was sent on a motor cycle with another despatch rider with Divisional Orders. These two successfully accomplished their mission though the enemy was apparently in Bayonvillers.

Meanwhile two officers despatched from B.H.Q. succeeded in reaching Fouilloy by skirting La Motte.

They brought with them a full report timed 10.50 p.m. on the 27th, from the Brigade as to the situation in front. The report stated that unless contrary orders were received arrangements would be made for the Infantry to extricate themselves by withdrawing in a South-westerly direction at 2 a.m. The report added that officers and men were exhausted by fatigue and lack of sleep.

The orders, however, carried by Lieut. Rorke, had meanwhile been received in the early morning and the two Brigades cancelled their scheme for withdrawing, and arranged to hold on to their present line and co-operate in the counter attack which was hoped would succeed in clearing the enemy from their rear.

At 1.30 a.m. on the 28th a further withdrawal to Cachy was ordered for the 134th Field Ambulance with its A.D.S. moved back to Villers Brettoneux, La Motte having been evacuated. The 132nd Field Ambulance was ordered to Domart and from thence via Boves to Sains en Amenois which was reached at 9 p.m. The unit stayed here until the afternoon of the 30th.

During this period the enemy's artillery and machine guns were very active and the order of battle was obscured. The 134th Field Ambulance was now clearing for many Divisions, all efforts being united to get back wounded irrespective of the formation to which they belonged. About this time the returns sent in by this unit showed casualties covering thirteen different Divisions apart from Corps and Army troops. It should also be noted at this point that all Divisional cars were now

Norfolk Bridge, Collecting Post

War Graves (*Post War*)
(*Showing those of* Barton, Brunger, *etc.*)

being placed at the disposal of the Ambulance working the line, and valuable assistance was also rendered by the Motor Ambulance Convoy.

Extra lorries were also obtained at different times provided by Q branch of the Division. And just before evacuating La Motte there were 120 wounded to be cleared, which seemed a physical impossibility. Q was informed of this and by means of a priority wire to Corps the transport was provided and not one of these men fell into enemy hands.

At 4 a.m. telephone orders were received from XIX Corps that a withdrawal was to be carried out immediately, before daylight if possible, to the line Vrely—Guillaucourt—Marcelcave. The two officers who had brought down news of the situation from the Brigades were therefore despatched by car at 4.30 a.m. with orders for all troops under Generals Armytage and Bellingham to withdraw via Harbonnieres—Caix-Cayeux to Ignaucourt, where they would be met with orders as to the line to be taken up.

Withdrawal commenced in full daylight at 7 a.m., the 117th Brigade moving first, their movements being covered by 118th Brigade. The enemy was not slow to notice this and put down a heavy and well directed barrage with artillery and machine guns, but fortunately did not inflict heavy casualties. He also advanced rapidly into Harbonnieres and forced a large number of men to keep in too westerly a direction. Brig.-Gen. Bellingham remained to supervise the right flank and rearguard of his Brigade, and with his Brigade Major, Major E. Gunner, D.S.O., was taken prisoner.

M

The 133rd Field Ambulance accomplished another move in sympathy with these retirements, proceeding to Hangard, and thence to Bois de Boves where they stayed until the 30th.

The G.O.C., G.S.O.2 and two officers of the Signal Company met the Brigades at Cayeux and Ignaucourt and gave them orders to occupy that portion of the line allotted to our Division, which ran from Marcelcave inclusive to Wiencourt inclusive.

The Divisional Commander personally supervised the placing of his troops along the new line. The line eventually taken up ran along the broad gauge railway running North of Marcelcave, to Weincourt. This line, however, was never securely established, owing to the continuous pressure exerted by the enemy and the uncertain position of Divisions on our right, who did not succeed in establishing a line Eastward towards Guillaucourt and Vrely.

Weincourt was soon found to be in the enemy's hands and a counter attack by the 116th and 118th Brigades, reorganised as Battalions, was arranged by the G.O.C. for its recapture. The manner in which the men, who were very tired through lack of sleep and food, advanced to the attack against heavy machine gun fire was excellent. They moved with the greatest steadiness and got in with the bayonet, killing many Germans and securing eight prisoners.

There were, however, no troops behind to support this advance, and Colonel Saint, 1/1st Cambridge-shire, who had taken over command of the remnants of 116th and 118th Brigades, decided to establish the line on the ridge running North from Cayeux where his right was in touch with French troops on the River Luce. The 117th Brigade during these operations occupied a position on the left, running North and South through the copse South of Bois de Pierret.

The three Brigades of Divisional Artillery, who had successfully carried out the withdrawal by the same route as the infantry, without loss, took up positions North-east of Aubercourt and South-east of Villers Brettoneux to cover the new line. During the carrying out of that retirement D.H.Q. had moved from Fouilloy to Domart sur la Luce.

The Headquarters of the 117th Brigade was established just North of Ignaucourt and those of 116th and 118th Brigades in Cayeux-en-Santerre. From this place the French line had been established running due South, whereas our line ran due West-nor-west, the village being in the angle. At about 4.30 p.m., the French troops withdrew to a line just in front of Ignaucourt leaving only a Cossack post on the East side of the village. The 118th Brigade was in touch with the French on their right but subsequently the latter moved back to Aubercourt. Notification of these moves by the French troops failed to reach Brigade or Division in both cases.

The 28th March was a moving day as far as the 134th Field Ambulance was concerned. No abiding place could be found and Cachy had to be evacuated for Aubercourt, the A.D.S. being established at Marcelcave. This move was accomplished at 11.30 a.m. Evacuation went on satisfactorily all day but toward midnight the attentions of the enemy became so pressing, the post being heavily shelled, machine-gunned and sniped and finally set on fire by an enemy shell, that the unit was compelled to move to Domart, the A.D.S. being now transferred to Aubercourt. Another move was necessary even from here and the Ambulance proceeded to Hangard.

During the afternoon of March 28th, the G.O.C. accompanied by G.S.O.1 again visited Marcelcave and the line thence to Aubercourt and placed Major Hesse, 1/6th Cheshire, in command of the troops holding the trenches, just East of the former village, with instructions to hold them to the last. A hostile demonstration against our left about 8 p.m. met with no success, the enemy was beaten off with loss and some prisoners remained in our hands. Hostile efforts to dislodge our patrols from Cayeux likewise failed and several prisoners, including one officer, were caught by our men.

At 10.30 p.m. the 118th Brigade with their right now exposed, decided to withdraw. Due notification was sent to the French and the 117th Brigade. The garrison of Cayeux formed a rearguard moving South of the River Luce. The remainder of the Brigade moved North of the river and by midnight had taken up a new position North-east of Aubercourt. To conform with this movement Brig.-Gen. Armytage, withdrew his troops to a line running from Aubercourt to Marcelcave in accordance with instructions previously issued by D.H.Q. in the event of such withdrawal being necessary.

A nucleus garrison under Brig.-Gen. Carey, known as Carey's Force, manned a line from Aubercourt through Marcelcave, and it was originally intended that our Division should withdraw behind this force and be ready to counter attack should the enemy establish himself in any part of the line.

The troops holding the line on the night of the 28th March were disposed as follows:—

117th Infantry Brigade with R.E. and Pioneers, on a line along the Demuin—Marcelcave Road. The 118th Brigade on the right continuing the line to the River Luce, and Carey's Force on the left holding the village of Marcelcave and extending the line Northwards. The Headquarters of Brigades were in the wood East of the Demuin—Villers Brettoneux Road.

The position about Marcelcave and South of the river was, however, very obscure, and before midnight, General Carey reported that the enemy were in Marcelcave, while the French had withdrawn West of Ignaucourt where there were elements of the 20th Division who should have been in touch with our right.

The night passed quietly and every endeavour was made to sort out units and to clear up the situation on our flanks. It was reckoned that the Division could not be counted on to find more than two Brigades each 350 all ranks strong.

March 29th was a bad day for our Division, though, except for slight shelling of our line, the day passed quietly. The enemy being more active against the Division on our right South of the river.

During the day both Domart and Hangard became
untenable for the medical units and a withdrawal
to Berteaucourt became necessary.   Here many
wounded were evacuated including a large number
of French casualties.   The bearers and M.T.
drivers did valiant work here all day and night.

About 12 noon whilst the G.O.C. and G.S.O.1
were walking up the main street of Demuin, the
enemy bombarded the village.   One shell burst in
a house they were passing and a splinter struck
Major-Gen. Feetham in the neck.   A medical
officer, attached to a Battalion of the Gloster
Regiment, assisted Lieut.-Col. Gosset to carry the
G.O.C., who was unconscious, clear of the village,
but from the first there was no hope.

Thus passed a very fine and fearless officer who was
beloved by all the Division.   His example and
keenness had been responsible in large measure for
the efficiency of the Division.   Scarcely a day had
passed, since he assumed command, without he
had gone to the foremost positions regardless of all
danger and thus stimulated, by personal example,
his men to maintain their positions and defeat the
enemy.   His body was brought back to Domart
and eventually handed over to the 132nd Field
Ambulance for safe keeping until arrangements
could be made for its burial.   A rough coffin
was made to enclose him.

At 12 noon the enemy launched an attack down the
valley of the Luce which was completely repulsed
by rifle and machine-gun fire.   Hostile batteries
galloping into action were thrown into confusion
by our fire.

The C.R.A., Brig.-Gen. W. G. Thompson, D.S.O., now assumed command of the Division.

At 4 p.m., orders were received from XIX Corps for the remnants of the Division to concentrate and hold a portion of the support line position about 1,000 yards West of Marcelcave. This line, when reconnoitred, was found to be unsuitable for concealing or accommodating troops during daylight, so units were finally assembled in the wood North-west of Aubercourt.

Carey's force was thus left responsible for the defence of the front line and our Division was in readiness to carry out any counter attack to restore the situation.

Considerable difficulty was experienced in sorting out the units and it was not until 6 a.m., the following morning that the concentration was complete. A readjustment of the artillery covering the Corps front also took place.

At 3.30 p.m., D.H.Q. moved from Domart to Boves.

At 7 a.m., March 30th, heavy shelling commenced along the Valley of the Luce and from 8 a.m. onwards troops were dribbling back from the Marcelcave—Aubercourt Line. General Armytage moved his units forward to occupy the spur South of the Bois de Hangard and a line running through the wood in which his B.H.Q. had been established. He moved his Headquarters further North towards Villers Brettoneaux.

At 11 a.m., the whole of our front line was apparently withdrawing. All men possible were stopped, reorganised by commanders on the spot and halted in the general line occupied by our Division.

During the morning the Headquarters of the 134th Field Ambulance withdrew to Boves leaving Berteaucourt as an A.D.S. Cars were now sent off in the direction of Cachy and Gentelles and a Collecting Post was established at the latter place. Wounded came in rapidly and continued on into the night. Touch with Brigade was maintained. At 9 p.m., all wounded were evacuated and personnel called in as the Division was being relieved. The main body of the 134th Field Ambulance proceeded to Guignemicourt at 11 p.m., having discharged their tour of duty with thoroughness, zeal and efficiency. In the latter stages of their journey this unit made splendid use of horsed ambulances far forward and for this received the personal commendation of the higher command. On this day also the 133rd Field Ambulance proceeded to Petitcagny near St. Fuscien. Here the personnel attached to the 134th Field Ambulance rejoined Headquarters and the unit finally came to rest in the Divisional Collecting Area at Bovelles. The 132nd Field Ambulance also moved from Sains en Amenois in the afternoon where it encamped in a brickfield, and after tea proceeded to Dury, and thence, via the mud, to Saleux. The next day it moved into the Divisional Collecting area near Bovelles, where it encamped in the open in pouring rain.

To retrace our steps slightly in order to carry on the narrative of the Division. At 1 p.m., a counter attack was organised by Brig.-Gen. Armytage and the enemy was driven back some 500 yards, offering very little resistance. Our troops, however, again fell back, and on again being reorganised, advanced against the enemy, but were unable to establish themselves in their original line.

At 2 p.m., cavalry reinforcements arrived and halted between the Bois de Hangard and the Wood to the East. Notification was also received from Corps that the Australians were to counter attack from the direction of Villers Brettoneaux with the objectives Aubercourt and the Copse 1,000 yards West of Marcelcave. These troops passed through the 39th Division about 4 p.m.

At the same time the 118th Brigade on the right of the 117th Brigade had been heavily engaged with the enemy from noon onwards. A counter attack organised by the Brigade Majors of the 116th and 118th Brigades, Capts. Tatham and Marr, succeeded in driving the enemy back in some confusion, but the ground gained could not be held for lack of support, and the Brigade finally withdrew to a line along the Canchy—Hangard Road. Intermittent fighting along the Bois de Hangard continued throughout the day.

About noon a warning order was received to the effect that the 18th Division would probably relieve all troops of the 39th and 66th Divisions in the line. Shortly after 7 p.m. orders were received from Corps that the relief would take place that night and the 18th Division would be moving up at dusk.

In the evening Major-Gen. Blacklock, C.M.G., D.S.O., arrived to take over command of the Division. Brig.-Gen. Thompson after handing over proceeded to Gentelles and reassumed command of the 39th Divisional Artillery.

The relief of the elements of our Division holding the line between Villers Brettoneaux and the Luce was carried out without incident and shortly after midnight G.O.'sC. 18th and 61st Divisions concurred in the withdrawal of the troops of the 39th Division. Our Division was now ordered to concentrate at Longeau where it was to await further orders. Arrangements were made to collect troops of the Division and to assist in guiding then to Longeau. All ranks were picketed and as soon as bodies of troops arrived, they were sorted out into units, given a hot meal and billeted in the village. It was not until late in the afternoon that the last element of the Division reached Longeau. After sorting out, each Brigade mustered just under 1,000 strong. The lorries of the M.T. Company were employed throughout the night of the 31/1st, conveying the troops to Guignemicourt and Dowelles. D.H.Q. moved from Boves to the Chateau at Guignemicourt at 2 p.m. in the afternoon of the 31st and the last lorry-load of troops left Longeau at 6 a.m. on April 1st. The Divisional Artillery remained in the line in the neighbourhood of Villers Brettoneaux. On April 1st, in the tiny cemetery of the village of Guignemicourt was laid to rest the body of the late G.O.C. of the Division. A very impressive though simple ceremony was carried out in according the last rites to one whose passing was sorely lamented by the Division. As officers slowly filed by the open grave, saluting for the last time their dead Commander, it seemed as though they were saluting the passing of the Division, as to all intents and purposes they were. The medical units were represented by 1 officer and 20 O.R's.

The retreat as a whole and in retrospect was perhaps the most remarkable experience we were called upon to pass through during our service. It commenced in the barren and stricken country about Gouzeaucourt and ended—as far as we were concerned—in the pleasantly wooded and fertile country West of Amiens. During that retro-gression we passed through an area hitherto un-touched by the War and were the witnesses of a pathos almost too deep for words. Pleasant home-steads, bereft of families, were left awaiting the marauders. The remains of a meal on the table, clothes hanging on the pegs. Young calves bleating in the barns awaiting their next meal, goats and bullocks wondering why their familiar friends were not there to satisfy their native hunger. In many cases we came upon the poor folk in the act of flight. What belongings could be done up in bundles were dumped into the capacious cart as the family jogged away to uncertainty and safety. Poorer folk, pathetic in their quiet sorrow, pushed some sort of a barrow, but all were united in the direction of their flight. In some cases, stolid in their fortitude, the family was grouped around the old fashioned stove, determined to await the oncoming foe. After all, war or no war, their home, their farmstead, was to them their world, and they were determined not to leave it even though their Europe weltered in conflict about them.

In too many cases, these pleasant little homesteads, these attractive Churches, were utterly destroyed by the avenging tide, and months later, when we visited this area again, we could hardly distinguish even the foundations of the places where so recently we had slept. The cheerful acquiesence, with what appeared to be the inevitable, was a noticeable characteristic of these quiet country folk so ruthlessly disturbed.

As far as we were concerned it must be confessed that we took refuge in the old adage concerning ill winds and made what comfort we could from an occasional chicken, a cheerful supply of eggs and sometimes a bottle of wine. Of a truth it was but little use to leave these things to a hungry foe when we, too, were too often hungry.

The Retreat was significant also of many things from the military point of view and the administrative side of the Medical Services. It was felt, and suitably represented to higher authority, that the R.M.O's. were not sufficiently co-ordinated in their work. Much greater value to the wounded would ensue, it was considered, if the R.M.O's were more intimately connected with the A.D.S's of the Ambulance evacuating the line. Time after time during the retirement R.M.O's lost touch with their units as owing to rapid changes in position it was impossible to establish R.A.P's or function them if established.

In the case of bearers, except for the first few days, it was found they were not able to pull their weight. Horsed and motor ambulances largely took their place, but these were all too insufficient in numbers. It was also considered that greater numbers, and an article of much lighter construction, should be available in the form of stretchers. The shortage of these essential articles was deplorable, something of so light a nature was needed that one man might carry three or four.

One significant fact remained, and reflected credit on the administration concerned, that the three Ambulances emerged from the Retreat intact, without loss of equipment, transport or personnel with one exception.

Mention has not been made concerning the movements of the A.D.M.S. which, of course, conformed with those of D.H.Q. Constant touch with the Ambulances was maintained, chiefly by means of despatch riders. The A.D.M.S. made his usual and daily visits to the source of evacuation. A feature of the operation was the large number of wounded dealt with at D.H.Q. The D.A.D's. M.S. time was fully occupied attending these and arranging for their evacuation.

The work of the R.M.O.'s was worthy of much praise. A shortage of stretchers was overcome by these officers improvising anything they could find from rifles to perambulators. Much of the work was actually done in the firing line and in many cases they were the last to withdraw to the new line.

The following letter from the Divisional General speaks for itself.

"Headquarters,
39th Division,
April 14th, 1918.

My dear Brazier-Creagh,

I have read with the greatest interest your report on the work of your department during the recent fighting in which the Division took part.

It is a story of achievement and success throughout, and on looking into the causes, the outstanding features, to my mind, are the thorough practical initial organisations, personal leadership, and that devotion to duty on the part of those under you, which wins us our fights.

It is difficult to single out anyone for special praise where all have played their part so well. Your Field Ambulance Commanders, their Assistants, the bearers, car drivers, despatch riders, and, we must not forget, the chaplains, of all denominations, who can and do great work on these occasions. All have done magnificently.

Troops fight best when they feel they are being thoroughly well looked after, and I want you to tell all your officers and men that therein they play a great and essential part in the winning of our fights. That the Division has always done what was asked of it is proof of the consistent good work of your department. Their success is due to knowing what was required of them, and how to do it—in other words, efficiency, and also to their devotion to duty, which in other words, means having the " go " and determination to put their training into effect under the difficult conditions of a modern battlefield.

It is very gratifying to me, on taking over command of the Division, to find your department, which is so essentially a part of its fighting machinery, on such a well ordered, firm footing.

> Believe me,
>
> Yours sincerely,
>
> (Signed) C. A. Blacklock."

During the retreat Private Mahoney of the 134th Field Ambulance was wounded and taken prisoner and Private McQueen wounded.

" Why, the figure is not even life-size! "
" But you know few men are life-size."

(Remark made by Scottish deputation
sent to purchase Whistler's portrait
of Carlyle, and Whistler's reply.)

The Wind-Jammers

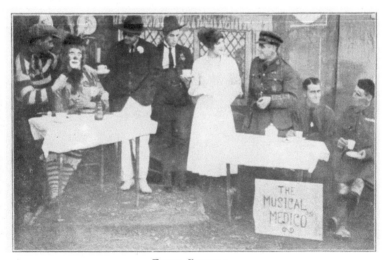

Folies Bergere

PERSONALIA

OUR Ambulances were composed of a cosmopolitan collection of men, as the opening sentences of this book would suggest. But a cleaner, nicer collection of youths, thrown together by the chances of War, could hardly have been found. Men from quite a number of walks in life found common ground and kinship. It was inevitable that like should meet like, but a mutual esteem grew up between the elements of our composition. The esteem for the complementary parts of character, lacking in one found in the other, thus making a homogeneous whole.

It is true we appeared to have no one of outstanding genius in the units, the ordinary person being largely in evidence, but we certainly had a variety of characters, individual in their idiosyncrasies and the expression of their life. These will come to mind again as we reflect in our respective ways of the men of whom we were once one.

Perhaps the section that most comes under criticism was the N.C.O's. These according to the tenets of Army routine were gifted with grey matter above their fellows, hence the responsibility that was theirs. It was interesting to watch the effect of military dignity conferred on this man and that by the advent of one stripe—with or without pay. Too often it was a heady wine! But of these, more anon.

Next in order of opprobrium, or praise, must come the cooks; although in reality these require a volume to themselves. If the words of that great Commander are true that " an Army marches on its stomach," then how large a part was played by these, the dirtiest men in the Ambulances. We speak physically rather than morally. Who can forget the stews they made and the water they spoiled. Yet we must offer them chaplets of abiding glory for the Christmas dinners they evolved, and which we so eagerly ate. And we must admit that all in all, conditions and rations being what they were, they served us well.

A little ditty that throws some light on the situation may not be out of place here.

> " We went to the Stores just to draw a few
> rations,
> We asked for a hundred of bread.
> But the Sergeant he barked and said, No,
> you can't have 'em,
> It's bully and biscuits instead."

That it was not always their fault is clearly denoted in the memorable occasion on which rice pudding was served up made with water, supplemented by figs without sugar. As no one could eat this the Q.M. arranged the next day for a bully beef stew and ordered the rice pudding that had been left over to be added as a thickener. But he forgot the presence of the figs!

And yet they were entirely responsible for the plum duff made from biscuits served up without the plums. This, boiled in new sandbags presented a somewhat hairy appearance when cooked. The great idea was to serve this with jam, but as there was not sufficient preserve to go round, two tins of jam were put in a dixie of hot water and served up as jam sauce.

And then there was the genial chef known to many as Dad P—. Never was he taken unawares and never could too many turn up unexpectedly to the feast. His great secret was to put another bucket of water in, and it was never known to fail. Then, too, there was the Corporal Cook, somewhat addicted to imbibing, who on one occasion upset a dixie of hot stew over himself. His confreres were rather amused when the M.O. applied picric acid to his rubicund face, thinking that was the affected part.

Turning from the culinary side to the regions of art and the drama, the 132nd Field Ambulance boasted a fully-fledged Concert Party known as the Mountebanks. A programme of which is immortalised here and now:—

1. Opening Chorus ... "The Mountebanks" ... ENTIRE COMPANY
2. Song ... ... "There's a Land" ... Sergt. H. WALLACE
3. Duet ... ... "Just another one" Privates F. A. GREAVES and J. McCOMBE
4. A Study from Life "The Game of Life" Sergt. J. V. HALLIDAY and Private W. GILBERT
5. Song ... ... "Nita Gitana" ... Private G. R. BROWN
6. Song ... ... "Proud I am" ... ... Sergt. H. WALLACE
7. Duet ... ... "Come under my umbrella" Privates G. R. BROWN and J. McCOMBE
8. Monologue... ... "Spotty" ... ... Sergt. J. C. HALLIDAY
9. Concerted Item ... "Dainty Flapper Girl" ... ENTIRE COMPANY
10. Song ... ... "I wanted to go back" Private S. C. SMITH
11. Song ... ... "Carmena" ... Private G. R. BROWN
12. Concerted Item ... "For me and my Girl" ENTIRE COMPANY

INTERVAL

SKETCH
A Theatrical Agents' Ordeal

A Theatrical Agent	...	...	...	...	Sergt. J. V. HALLIDAY
His Valet	...	...	...	...	Private F. A. GREAVES
A Texas Sharpshooter	...	...	...	...	L/Corpl. J. R. STOKER
A Would-be Actress	...	...	...	...	Private J. McCOMBE
A Fallen Star	...	...	...	...	Sergt. J. V. HALLIDAY
An Elocutionist	...	...	...	...	Private T. SIDGEWICK
A Melodramatic Actress	...	...	...	...	Private W. GILBERT
P.C. GLAXO	...	...	...	...	...	L/Corpl. T. VASS

Whilst the 134th Field Ambulance also boasted a Concert Party under Corporal P. Shaw, that made a name for itself, not least amongst the W.A.A.C's. And the 133rd Field Ambulance a famous band that ploughed a way for the unit through the Hindenberg Line! alleging that it was " the first that ever burst upon that silent sea."

It is pleasant, too, to remember the attachment which sprang up between the drivers of the A.S.C. attached to us, and their horses and mules. One recalls the day when he had to hand over his " four-legged pals " to the Americans at Watten and was certain that they shed tears, as he did, at the parting. Whilst another states that his pair of mules could pick their way anywhere, even through the eye of a needle! And what great friends they were to him! The N.C.O.'s, especially the Sergeant-Majors, of these transports, are held in kindly memory by those who had to do with them.

Water-cart orderlies, too, have been mentioned as deserving of praise, one in particular, B.S., described as small of stature, but large of heart, always cheerful, ever at work, seeking to do a little kindness for this man and that. Not a bad record or character for any man, either in peace or war.

But to return to the N.C.O.'s. First comes a man
straight and tall, with large voice, but slender
education, who must be marked out for promotion.
So certain and so swift was the process of his
elevation that he became a living example of that
frog who sought to illustrate the immensity of the
ox. He became a Sergeant-Major, but burst by
virtue of his own office.

Then comes to mind a little Lance-Corporal of
sanitary instincts, who, by virtue of his stripe,
thus possessing the necessary acumen above his
fellows, found himself Ward Master for one brief
night at a large hospital which the Ambulance
was then running for mild medical and surgical
cases. It is true he could hardly be described as
second to none in " the strokes of the pen or turn
of wit," but in the few hours of his clinical authority
he managed to mix up contagious diseases with the
ordinary patients to the consternation of the M.O.
in the morning. He was, therefore, relieved from
further medical control of this order.

And we must not forget the Sergeant who was an
excellent dresser, but who suffered a sad impediment
in his speech. So afflicted was he that his whole
body vibrated to his speech with too often distressing
results. His speciality was the administration of
anti-tetanic serum, given to every wounded man.
Holding the somewhat dreadful-looking syringe at
" the ready," he would say, " Ju-u-u-st a p-p-p-prick
chum," but ere the last word was out, his body
had lunged forward and several inches of needle
had entered the unsuspecting epidermis!

Perhaps his best effort was on a very dark night in a certain camp that was built on piles. An officer patient stopped him, with an enquiry, on the duck-board track some two feet above ground level, so emphatic was the reply and with such labour, that the officer was amazed to find his informer had suddenly disappeared into the darkness. He had fallen off the track into the mire.

Yet another was a Sergeant with soft and lady-like manners suggestive of the young ladies' academy rather than the aggression of the barrack room. His nightly visitation of " lights out " at Eastbourne was more of a caress than a command. A delightful youth in many ways, yet one of the greatest contradictions in life. He could speak French like a native and drink wine like a fish, so much so that a stomach pump had to be used on one occasion to save his life. Too great also was his capacity for making friends of the wrong type. His decline and subsequent death was a sadness to those who knew him.

There were, of course, more men than N.C.O.'s in the Ambulances and these must be left to the memories of their friends and admirers. We can but recall one or two.

First, the man who had double-jointed hips and would amuse his comrades ere they slept and when times were quiet, by his impossible antics. He could scratch his ears with his own toes and manipulate his legs in such fashion as to suggest the frog or ape rather than the man.

Another was a short, choleric-looking private, no longer a youth, who had an unfortunate nose. He was always the first to make his bed in the sleeping chamber and the first asleep. His snoring was of such persistency that boots and other things had to be thrown before others could woo " tired nature's sweet restorer."

There was another, round and fat and jolly, with a capacity for caricature, who evidently bore about his person the seeds of incipient diabetes. His continual hunger, his capacity for the eating of " erfs " and yet withal his cheerful smile were a marvel to us all. His career was cut all too short by an enemy bomb dropped on one of the hospitals.

Then another who bore a pleasant name but a sallow complexion, who also could do justice to one meal or two. His occupation in the piping times of peace was thrower-out at one of the London Music Halls.

Yet another was one of those heavy, mysterious types, whose capacity for gambling was immense. He ran a crown-and-anchor board, was in funds and out, and was once seen walking the streets of Amiens very drunk, holding a watch in one hand and a bundle of notes in the other. When the Ambulances were finally disbanded and marched out from Etaples in two's and three's to join other units, he was last seen bidding a farewell to his erstwhile comrades from the bars of the military prison there.

One came from the land of wizardry and was a regular. Like those of his compeers who soldiered before the advent of War he knew how to take care of himself. He was somewhat addicted to the acquisition of souvenirs, especially from German prisoners. A suggestion once made to him that a prisoner who had just been placed in an Ambulance was hiding something under his tongue had the desired effect. He must needs make the poor enemy open his mouth, lest like the oyster, it should contain a pearl.

The following personal reminiscences from a member of one of the Ambulances are of considerable interest. He states that he was the baby of the unit, having enlisted at $16\frac{3}{4}$ years, and was only 17 when the Ambulance proceeded overseas. He was amongst the first to win the M.M. and bore a charmed life, as the following will suggest:—

" When Bethune was being shelled in 1916, I was one who volunteered to go out into the town. We paraded in the schoolyard, but just before going out, the officer put P. Brown in my place. He was killed.

September 3rd. Was detailed to a stretcher squad by Capt. Lindeman, but afterwards was detailed to stay in the communication trench to direct walking wounded. The man put in my place had a machine gun bullet through the lung.

At Passchendaele Ridge I was runner to Capt. Limbery and had been out with him on several occasions during that day. He told me to find a funk hole and have a rest, taking another man with him. It was their last journey!

Was knocked over by the same shell that wounded T., without getting a scratch.

Was on the same stretcher squad as H.T. at Tower Hamlets. We were called out of the dug-out to take a case down, when for some reason H.T. did not come out and somebody else took his place. We had only gone a short distance when the dug-out was hit."

Yet another writes to say what a fraternal spirit existed amongst the men and how the older men, when up the line, would go out time after time in order to let the youngsters stay in comparative safety.

There was also the case of the canny Newcastle chap who was sleeping with his comrades in a barn adjacent to a cesspool. He had been imbibing somewhat freely and found it necessary to pay several calls outside. On one of these excursions he mistook his footing and accidentally fell into the pool. The resulting mess was so awful that he had to divest himself of all his clothing and came back as naked as Cupid. This, much to the amusement of his comrades except those who were sleeping close to him as he had by no means rid himself of the smell.

Finally, there comes the story of the man who was found lying in the road and was thought to have been run over. Two men carried him in and proceeded to undress him, when he began to vomit. When the M.O. arrived he asked, " Has he brought up much blood? " " No, sir," replied the orderly, " only stout ! "

That, of course, we had officers whose peculiarities and individual touches were well known to us cannot be gainsaid. In fact, these might be classified under the headings of Good, Bad and perfectly B . . . . . y.

First comes an officer, past the first flush of youth, somewhat portly, who would ride his charger. To ride was one thing, to mount another. To accomplish the latter he must needs borrow a box. The charger having been brought alongside, the officer mounts the box. The hoss, evidently an old soldier, looks round, sees the avoirdupois about to mount his back and moves three paces forward!

Another is an officer with thin and horse-like legs who wears a monocle and adopts a lisp. Is it to be wondered he is known as Algernon? How he loved to perform marvellous evolutions on the parade ground with the men of his section. How too, was he renowned for losing himself and us, when out on route march. His appeals to us not to " whander all over the pahwish " were inimitable. But all will agree that he was a jolly good sort.

One was an officer-commanding whose *alma mater* was Cambridge. His capacity for regulations amounted to a fine form of ritual and suggested he should have been in the Church rather than the Army. Yet he was a regular.

Another officer-commanding, a poor sleeper at night, had seen much service in India. The amount of work he extricated from his men and the fear which he inspired in the hearts of his N.C.O.'s suggested a closer acquaintance with a race of another colour than our own.

Then comes Captain Mac, a gentleman in every respect. Very kindly disposed to the patients, particularly the younger ones. A frequent question was, "When does this lad's unit return to the line?" "The day after to-morrow, sir!" "Very well, give him another day and then he will miss a turn in the trenches." Despite his quiet and kindly way he could soon pick out a shirker, who was quickly marked for duty.

Sport entered a good deal into the life of the Ambulances and many Football and Cricket Matches were played, when the units were out on rest or in quiet pastures, that remain a pleasant memory with those who took part. Some of these have found mention in the chronicle of events though in a somewhat bald and uninformative manner.

We are indebted to a correspondent for the following:—

"We had in our ranks a fine array of footballers, and many were the exciting matches played, not only amongst ourselves, but against neighbouring units, when facilities were afforded. Our football was ubiquitous and no part of the Quartermaster's Stores was guarded so jealously and packed so securely when we were on the march as the leather sphere which played so large a part in the life of the men when at rest!"

But it is with the cricket exploits that these notes taken from a private diary, are chiefly concerned:—

"On August 11th, 1917, at the then lovely village of Meteren, near Bailleul, a match was played between officers and N.C.O.'s on the one hand and the humble privates on the other, which resulted in a win for the latter by 33 runs to 4!" The sole entry in the diary after the score is that " It was a fine game." For whom? one wonders!

When the unit moved to Chippewa Camp of happy and unhappy memory, several matches were played against an R.F.A. and A.S.C. unit with no recorded results.

Our greatest cricket feast, however, was at Bollezeele Camp, a beautiful spot in which we were privileged to stay for several weeks, during July and August of 1918. Perhaps some details of the games played here may be interesting to our readers.

A match was played on July 31st, between the Ambulance and an A.O.C. unit, which we won by 66 runs to 36. A few days later, on August 4th, came a great match with a Corps School, whose team included none other than W. J. Abel of Surrey fame, and a son of the great Bobbie. It is hardly necessary to state that W. J. proved much above our class, and the match went against us by 88 to 37. When it is observed, however, that Abel scored 52 and claimed nine wickets for six runs, it will surely be acknowledged that the remaining members of the team had little say in the matter. A piquant incident in this game must be recorded.

The writer well recollects opening the innings for the Ambulance with a dapper little chap from Northampton who, completely unperturbed by the fame of the man who was bowling to him (Abel), off-drove his first ball beautifully to the boundary for four! But this was obviously too good to last, as the result given above shows, and the next ball shattered his wicket in no uncertain manner.

Our next match on August 8th, was against some Canadian Railway troops, who were not quite up to Test Match standard, as the diary entry tells us they were exceedingly poor at the game. The scores, 112 to 12, in favour of the Ambulance, would appear to justify this candid statement.

Now let us turn to another match which had been looked forward to most eagerly and this was with another Field Ambulance of our Division, who had the reputation of being very hot stuff. Our boys, however, were tuned up to concert pitch and in their very best form and we won with somewhat unexpected ease by 88 runs to 22. Another interval of two days and we found ourselves opposed to the 108th Field Ambulance, who proved to be a remarkably good all-round team, and we had to acknowledge defeat to the tune of 77 runs to 51. Another match played whilst at Bollezeele was between the unit and a large batch of reinforcements that had lately arrived. After a most enjoyable afternoon, the teams and spectators were highly diverted to see on the notice board an announcement that, " Dr . . . . . the great bonesetter, had kindly promised to referee the match, and in order to do so had declined an invitation to lecture to the Royal Society on ' The application of the Thomas's Splint.' It was felt that, such generosity deserved recognition and the doctor was to be presented with a case of hair brushes and a cask of hair oil." It should be mentioned that the " Doctor " was a man who took immense pride in his personal appearance, who spent most of his spare time in bathing and anointing himself and was reputed to carry a dressing gown in his pack.

We cannot, however, leave the delectable Bollezeele without mentioning another great sporting event which occurred there. No event in the unit's history created more interest and fun than the running match arranged between B. and J. It is only necessary to say that the first-mentioned was a hospital orderly and the second, the incomparable laundryman of the Ambulance. Exact details of the contest are not available, but it certainly emanated from a challenge. On a glorious evening in July, 1918, every available man, and many officers, were at the starting post to see these two, immaculately attired in vests, shorts and running pumps, get off the mark. Many of the fellows accompanied the runners over the course, but some of the less energetic, excitedly awaited the return of J. and B., speculating as to whether J., a much older man than B., would be able to stick the pace and finish the course. This he did, most bravely, but, as was expected, victory went to the man with youth on his side. This little contest was the sole topic of conversation for many days.

Several games of cricket were indulged in whilst the units were at Rouen, whilst there was always the popular and simply arranged ring tennis. Billiards were enjoyed, too, at many of the Church Army and other Huts provided for the amelioration of the soldier's lot!

From all of which it would be concluded that War was not sufficiently powerful with all its horror and misfortune to destroy that essential portion of a man's being—his spirit. Expressed more widely in the somewhat hackneyed phrase, " Esprit de Corps! "

" Above all, no reproaches about what is past and cannot be altered! How can a man live at all if he did not grant absolution every night to himself and all his fellows! "

GOETHE.

EPILOGUE

IT may seem strange to the general reader that the account from now onwards should be headed as an epilogue. We have left the enemy at the gates and so much remains to be done ere we write Finis to the story. The following letter, however, addressed to Gen. Sir H. C. O. Plumer, G.C.B., G.C.M.G., G.C.V.O., A.D.C., in whose Army we spent so much time, and were destined to spend yet more, will explain much:

" G.H.Q.,
British Armies in France,
14th July, 1928.

The heavy fighting which has taken place since the 21st March, and the question of man-power generally has rendered it impossible to maintain all the units which were in the field when the operations commenced this Spring.

Some Battalions have, therefore, been reduced to Battalion Training Staffs, while some have been or will be disbanded entirely.

I fully realise how deeply officers and men will feel the reduction or disbandment of battalions with which they have been so closely connected and with which they have fought with such energy, gallantry and success in the past, and I know that since this reorganisation is unavoidable, all ranks will accept it with the loyalty and devotion which has been so conspicuous during every trial throughout the War.

I therefore wish you to convey to the officers, N.C.O.'s and men of these battalions my deep regret that this step should have been found necessary and my great appreciation of the valuable service that Battalion Training Staffs are now rendering to the Allied cause in perfecting the fighting power of the American Troops; and further to inform them that units are not selected for reduction or disbandment because they have fought any less gallantly than those still existing, but solely on account of the impossibility of their maintenance.

(*Signed*) D. Haig, F.M."

Having arrived at Bovelles and concentrated ourselves in the area, we again proceeded to march. On April 2nd, the 132nd Field Ambulance marched some fifteen miles to Araines and on the next day another fifteen miles to Focaucourt, where the unit rested until the 7th. On this day it again marched to Frettemeule and on the 8th to Oust-Mares. The 9th saw it reach the entraining centre of Eu. These marches were particularly pleasant as they led through scenes pleasantly contrasting with those we had just passed. We marched on, away from war into the peace of a serene and beautiful countryside. Wooded hills and valleys, nestling villages, fields tilled and sown towards a coming harvest. Everywhere was cleaner, sweeter, more alluring than we had known for many days. The green of Spring, the freshness of new-turned earth, inspired us with other hopes and new vigour. We now came in contact with simple folk to whom the War had but little significance. They looked with wonder at this advent of troops, though many of the older ones remembered 1870 and all the significance of fateful days.

In like manner the 133rd Field Ambulance marched to Avel Esques on April 2nd and Fresne-Tilloy near Oisemont the next day, where a hospital was established and a visit from the new G.O.C. of the Division made. On the 7th the unit marched to Hocquelus and on the 9th the entraining point of Woincourt was reached.

The 134th Field Ambulance proceeded to Halli-villiers on the 2nd, and to Fresnoy-Andainville the next day. Here the G.O.C. also paid a visit of inspection on the 4th. On the 7th a march of nine-teen miles to Dargnies was accomplished and the next day the unit entrained at Eu.

One night in the train—a sufficiency, as all who partook of those journeys will agree—and we were at our detraining stations. The 132nd Field Ambulance arrived at Arques on the 10th and later marched to Watten, while the 133rd Field Ambulance detrained at St. Omer and proceeded to Moulle to a general hospital where they stayed for the night. The 134th Field Ambulance also detrained at Arques and marched to Longueness, while on the 11th it proceeded to Berthem.

Barely here and the tide of War must needs draw us back. As this record discloses there were still some remnants of our Division left. These, after having been collected together and sorted out, were formed into what was known as the 39th Division Composite Brigade and attached to the XXII Corps. This done they were rushed up once more into the old familiar Salient where the line had given way by the Portuguese, necessitating the withdrawal by the whole of the Second Army. The honours of more line work now fell to the 133rd Field Ambulance.

This unit was actually on the line of march the next day for Moulle when a motor cycle despatch rider overtook them. The instructions were to dump kits, put on helmets and fall in. In less time than it takes to tell they were back in St. Omer entraining for the North. Some hours later the unit detrained at Vlamertinghe, so well known to them by reason of its Mill. Headquarters were established at Scottish Lines and the unit proceeded to move in Battle order. The Compositive Brigade was attached to the 21st Division in General Plumer's Second Army. Most of the transport of the Ambulance was left at Monnecove Moulle.

The first three or four days was spent moving about from camp to camp and on the 12th the unit moved to Manchester Camp, into which a shell was dropped at night, and on the 14th to La Clytte Camp. Whilst on the 15th it moved to Waratah Camp and from here 16 O.R.'s were sent to the Forward area. On the 20th Major H. J. de Brent, Lieuts. Bardal and Egan with a bearer party took over a Collecting Post at Voormezeele and Spoil Bank and proceeded to evacuate the line for the 21st Brigade, 30th Division, now attached to the 21st Division. This

Brigade had relieved a Brigade of the 9th Division. Heavy fighting was reported about Kemmel and Kemmel Hill on March 25th, while the next day the enemy captured Spoil Bank about 9.30 a.m., which necessitated the evacuation of Voormezeele. Woodcote House was now opened as a Main Collecting Post, cases being brought back by Swan Chateau to Belgian Battery Corner by bearers and thence to Trinity A.D.S. by car. Larch Wood and Rutledge Post continued to function.

On the night of the 26/27th April, our line was withdrawn to one just East of Ypres and on this day the officer in charge of Woodcote House and the personnel, also those from Rutledge Post and Larch Wood rejoined their unit, the evacuation of this portion of the line having been handed over to the 64th Field Ambulance of the 21st Division. On April 30th Lieut. G. H. Boyer and a bearer sub-division were sent to Vijverhoek to work the right sector of the 21st Divisional Front. Later a second bearer sub-division was also sent. The men proceeded to Dickebusch by 'bus, where an old chateau was taken over as a Dressing Station. Here the time was spent in the cellar awaiting their turn to go up the line. The way led by Cafe Belge towards Voormezeele Brasserie. The roads were torn by shell fire and the air reeked with the pineapple-like smell from exploding gas shells. A barricade was erected across the road at this point. Under cover of darkness the men arranged themselves into stretcher parties, climbed the barricades and proceeded to carry down the wounded. The darkness was intense and the way difficult, so difficult in fact, that too often the sufferers were shot completely off the stretchers as the bearers fell into the shell holes. In the morning the R.A.P. was moved down to the Chateau and the carry was from thence to Belgian Battery Corner, a distance of nearly two miles. The bearers were kept busy and allowed no rest, the work involving seven or eight cases per party in twelve hours. This resolved itself into a walk of twenty-eight miles, to say nothing of the dead weight on the stretcher for half that distance. This work was carried on under exceedingly heavy fire, but the ground being soft from the spring rains the splinters of the bursting shells were but few and the casualties small.

Lieut. Boyer, who was attached to our Division from the American Army, was a man with a philosophical contempt of death. Nothing flurried him or made him afraid. Himself fearless, he was exacting towards the bearers under his charge, but such a man could not but win respect.

The Headquarters of the 133rd Field Ambulance had now moved to Remy Sidings, and a Walking Wounded Post was established at Waratah Camp under Major Warwick. Lieut. Boyer and his party returned to Headquarters on the 2nd May, having experienced a short and sharp term of service. The party proceeded by small trucks on the light railway to Waratah Camp and, after a meal, to Remy Sidings. The shelling at this time was amongst the most intense experienced and that the unit did not sustain more casualties is little short of miraculous.

An incident occurred at this time which is worthy
of note. Amongst those who were sent with Lieut.
Boyer was a man of very high principles whose
worth was greatly appreciated by the few who
knew him. He had made friends with and
chaperoned a man younger than himself, and with
whom he had but little in common, owing to a
promise made to the lad's mother when he enlisted.
This boy was reported wounded to this man, who
was awaiting his turn with others to go out on a
bearer party. Nothing loath and without hesitation,
he went in search of his friend, and was killed in
the act. A simple devotion, brooking no memorial,
but significant of that Greater Love. The boy,
incidentally, had been but slightly wounded in the
knee.

A congratulatory message was received from the
Major-Gen. Commanding the 21st Division as
follows:—

" Well done, the 39th Division. You have done
splendid work under the most adverse circumstances
and I am sure you will continue to do so whenever
your services are required. I fully realise what you
have been through and cannot express my admiration for the behaviour of all ranks.

(Signed) David J. M. Campbell."

The following two letters also speak for themselves
and need no comment.

" A.D.M.S., 21st Division.

Will you please accept my congratulations to
yourself and the officers and other ranks R.A.M.C.
under your command on the extraordinarily efficient

manner in which casualties have been evacuated
from your area under the recent trying conditions.
I have never seen the work more speedily and
successfully carried out.

(Signed) C. Begg,
May 1st, 1918.   XXII Corps,
Colonel D.D.M.S."

" O.C., 133rd Field Ambulance.

In forwarding the letter of the D.D.M.S., XXII
Corps, I wish to express my high appreciation
of the work done by yourself and the officers and
men of your unit, and to thank you and them for
the courage they have shown, and the assistance
they have rendered while working with the 21st
Division.

(Signed) D. O. Hyde, Colonel A.M.S.,
May 3rd, 1918.   A.D.M.S., 21st Division."

On April 5th, the 133rd Field Ambulance entrained
at Remy Sidings for Autingues. April 14th brought
news that a very popular officer of this unit, Capt. S.
J. L. Lindeman, who had always been considered
part and parcel of its make up, though he had been
away for many months as R.M.O., had been
awarded the M.C. for bravery in the Field. On
the 17th news was also received by the unit that
the M.M. had been awarded to Sergt. Wishart,
R.A.M.C., and Privates Cousins and Connor, of
the M.T., A.S.C.

It is necessary now to slightly retrace our steps to
the other Ambulances whom we left amid the apple
blossoms of the St. Omer district. The 132nd Field
Ambulance had established a hospital at Watten

and were the first of our Division to receive admissions from the American Expeditionary Force, but lately arrived in France. On the 15th April, 4 O.R.'s of the 77th American Division were admitted to hospital. The Tivolies, the Divisional Concert Party, paid a welcome visit to this unit on April 22nd, when a most enjoyable evening was spent. Both the A.D.M.S. and the D.A.D.M.S. took part in this festival.

Whilst at Berthen the 134th Field Ambulance was called upon to enquire into the loss of rifles by the A.S.C. attached. One of those frequent but somewhat unproductive processes that were indulged in by Army formations. Evidently the losses had been sustained during the retreat. On April 29th a somewhat ambiguous entry in the War diary states that 40 men of this unit were entertained from 6 to 8.30 at Audricq by members of the W.A.A.C.

May was a month of somewhat chequered memory as far as the medical units of our Division were concerned. The 132nd Field Ambulance received news on the 4th that the M.M. had been conferred on two A.S.C. men, viz.:

0/1030 Sergt. E. S. Stinchcombe, A.S.C., M.T.
M2/132732 Private D. C. Kay, A.S.C., M.T.

And again on the 25th, that Sergt. Stinchcombe had been mentioned in Despatches. On the 11th this unit handed over its hospital to the 306th Ambulance Corps of the 306th Field Hospital of the 77th American Division, who were now preparing to take their part in the struggle.

The 133rd Field Ambulance had established a hospital in the Chateau at Autingues, a beautiful little spot some ten miles from Calais. One of the principal inhabitants here was an Englishman who owned a lace factory in Calais, while many of the village folk earned their living in the seaport. A dirty little train, so characteristic of France and Flanders, passed through these meadows on its way to Calais and the folks boarded the train in the midst of the cornfields. No shops were here, no attractions, simply peace and the pleasures of the countryside. Not far was a forest which stretched for miles, the home of wild boars who sometimes came sniffing around the back doors early in the morning. The country and its villages were but little changed since Wordsworth came into these parts a wild and revolutionary young man. But then were the days of the French Revolution. Guns could be faintly heard in the distance, while enemy planes could be heard at night droning their way to Calais.

A band, of which the unit had become a proud possessor, first came into being here and used to take the remainder of the Ambulance on route marches. What the local people thought is not recorded.

A fortnight of real rest and recreation was spent amid these ideal surroundings. The weather was turning warm, and with tolerable food, clean clothes, facilities for bathing and washing, and a pleasant association with the simple village folk, many considered that the time spent here was amongst the happiest of all the days abroad. Especially

welcome was it as a contrast to the periods that had
been passed through in the Retreat and again at
Voormezeele.

At the close of this rustication the Field Ambulance
held their Sports on May 19th, when a very happy
day was spent in ideal weather. The events included
100, 400, 440 yards, pillow fights, veterans' race,
tug of war, long jump, hurdle race, sack race,
wrestling on horseback, etc. The prizes were
presented by the A.D.M.S. in his usual breezy
and fatherly manner. The whole village turned out
to enjoy the occasion and the coloured frocks of the
village maidens added an attractive background to
the scene. A cup for the largest number of points
gained was won by Private Williams.

Much talk and many rumours had been circulating
as to our ultimate destiny as a Division. The
Retreat had hit us badly and it seemed as though the
remnants had been collected together and thrown
into the melting pot at Voormezeele to complete
the disintegration. Be that as it may it was decided
to reduce the 39th Division to cadre strength as
a training staff for the new American Divisions now
taking the field.

Accordingly, with heavy hearts and much sadness
of farewell, the 132nd and the 134th Field Ambulance
personnel took leave of their fellows who had been
selected to remain with the Headquarters of their
units and proceeded to Audricq on May 12th to
entrain for the Base Depot at Rouen. It was not
until a week later, the day following their Sports,
that the 133rd in like manner, marched a hot and

dusty way to Audricq in order to entrain for the same place. Friendships had sprung up between these men which, it was feared, were all too soon to be broken.

The journey to Rouen was a pleasant one through undulating country at a season when the weather was kind and made one feel how good it was to be alive. Great activity appeared on the railways in the number of troop trains we passed, especially those of French units dressed in their native blue and replete with wine flasks.

Arrived at Rouen towards evening, we marched through the town to the Cyclists' Base Depot and were soon accommodated in tents amid this busy throng. Some Divinity still seemed to be shaping our end, for we were not dispersed to the four winds as we imagined would be our fate, but retained in our respective units. It was not long before we realised with great joy that we were not to be broken up after all.

Henceforward, and for the six weeks we were destined to be here, we settled down to enjoy the amenities of Rouen and district. Our occupation consisted of fatigue at the various Base and Stationary Hospitals, and we were destined to see even a seamier side of War in the quiet, sustained suffering of those broken men. Funeral parties had to be provided, which was a wretched job owing to the sometime attendance of relatives of the deceased from home. Fatigues for the operating theatre, a still more distressing job owing to the atmosphere and the stertorous breathing of the patients, and the attendance on men wounded in varying degrees. Some were sad enough in the conditions to which they had been reduced, whilst others were sadder still in that they had no friends, no relations and no wish to recover. However, we scrubbed wards, floors of huts as big as fields, and attended to the various kinds of sanitation so necessary to the well-being of a closely concentrated civilisation.

In spare moments, of which, be it thankfully recorded, there were many, we paid official and unofficial visits to the city. Boarded the penny trams that plied there, hung on as it were by our teeth, crowded round the driver, and paid up willingly to the feminine conductor. Once in Rouen we kept out of the way of Military Police as far as possible, enjoyed the Cathedral and Ruskin's little gem of St. Maclou, the great clock that spanned the little street, and paid tribute to that Divinity of Womanhood in the person of St. Joan. We saw the place of her incarceration, her death, and the memorial at Bon Secour erected by a nation that had traduced and spurned her genius. To say nothing of restaurants, estaminets, shops, and all the glories of a city away from the line.

We were not left entirely in peace, however, as the air raid menace followed us down, and we were soon set to work digging trenches into which the troops might take shelter. This was indeed hard work, as just below the surface was an exceedingly hard and impermeable strata that required the modern pneumatic drill rather than the hand shovel. Our sleep, too, was disturbed by various raid alarms, real or imaginary, too often the latter. Some of us tried to burk these tocsins, considering death and sleep the more welcome, but we were successfully turfed out of our blankets ere the authorities were satisfied.

Whilst we were rusticating at Rouen the Headquarters of our Ambulances were having an equally good time in the pleasant country behind Calais. The 132nd Field Ambulance, which now consisted of the O.C., the Q.M. and 22 O.R., proceeded to Burnonville on June 20th, in order to train the 311th Ambulance Co. Field Hospital of the 78th American Division. During the time spent here the Ambulance sustained a great loss when on June 26th, the O.C., Lieut.-Col. A. Littlejohns, was admitted sick to the 44th Field Ambulance and evacuated. Colonel Littlejohns had been with the unit through all its vicissitudes from the days at Twezeldown. The next day the Headquarters proceeded to Abbeville in order to re-equip and prepare for the welcome business of receiving the lost sheep in the return of its personnel so lately sent to the Base in tears. The Headquarters now under the command of Major Morris shared with the 112th Field Ambulance, the Chinese Camp, at Moutort. The M.S.M. was awarded to 65795 Sergt. A. C. Piper during this month.

The cadre establishment of the 133rd Field Ambulance sustained a loss, as did the whole Ambulance, when goodbye had to be said on May 25th, to Major S. J. L. Lindeman who was transferred to the A.D.M.S., 6th Division, on this date. Major Lindeman was an extremely popular officer with the unit, whose destinies and fortune he had watched over from its birth. Indeed he had been, in some measure, responsible for the accouchement. The Ambulance owed him a considerable debt and was not slow to acknowledge its obligation. On June 22nd the A.D.M.S. held an investiture when he presented the ribbons of the D.S.O. to Lieut.-Col. Sinclair Miller, and the M.S.M. to Sergt.-Major Herbert, and the D.C.M. to Sergt. Peel. On June 26th the Headquarters of this unit also proceeded to Abbeville on the welcome journey of meeting their old friends and being refitted.

The 134th Field Ambulance as a training cadre, proceeded to Mondicourt on May 15th and from there marched to Pas in order to instruct the 305th American Field Ambulance in the British method of recording evacuations, together with the use of equipment. On June 10th, they again moved to Berthen and on the 19th to Viel Moutier, in order to receive the 312th Field Ambulance, American Army for similar instruction. June 26th saw the Headquarters march to Desures where it entrained for Abbeville, also for the welcome purpose of re-equipping and the re-union with severed friends. It is a tribute to the spirit which existed in the Ambulances that in all the cases of re-union they were looked upon as the happiest occasions the Ambulances had known. It was also but an enlargement of the spirit which prompted casualties when once recovered to get back to their units if at all possible. Wherever the unit might be and in whatsoever conditions, there was home and the friends that had proved themselves to be of such worth.

As far as the irresponsible body of O.R.'s was concerned, they heard with joy the news they were to rejoin their respective units. Those for the 132nd arrived at Abbeville from Rouen on June 28th, met their friends and picked up the baggage that was so dear to them. The 133rd and the 134th personnel had arrived at Abbeville the day previously and were only too pleased so to do.

A night or two was spent here in various camps and we took the opportunity of having a good look round the ancient town. We found the place very deserted owing to the constant air raids, and signs of damage were apparent on every hand. However, we did not forget to visit the Collegiate Church of St. Wulfram, with its twin towers and their mediæval vanes. At night we saw the balloons rising round the city which, with with their nets, were proving to be an effective barrier to the enemy aircraft. Certainly no raiders appeared whilst we were there.

July 1st saw the whole of the Ambulances report to the R.T.O. Triage, where they entrained for the rural amenities of Audricq. We were up betimes, somewhere about 4.30 and were despatched with some rapidity, resulting in our arrival at Etaples in the afternoon. Here we detrained and marched into this famous centre of camps and hospitals. Our arrival could hardly be forgotten. As we marched in we saw remains of last night's air raid, heard terrible tales of things past, and were ushered into a square, surrounded by tents that had been revetted against bomb splinters. Here we were harangued by the Camp Sergt.-Major in the following terms. " In the event of an air raid you will stay in your tents. You will be perfectly safe unless a bomb falls on the tent, then you won't know anything about it." Sixteen to a tent! how uncomfortable. One or two mustered a grouse to their friends, but these, being wise in their campaigning, suggested waiting and seeing. Night came, only four in the tent, where were the other twelve? They had gone to the adjacent woods rather than be sheltered and protected by government tents. Towards morning the intermittent drone, unmistakable in its unfriendly nature, and soon the far distant thunder of dropping charges. Result, a very good night for those in the tents, a certainly broken rest for those in the woods and a plentitude of falling splinters between the trees.

The next morning, however, we were off again, made our way to the station, reported to the R.T.O., New Sidings, and were soon at Audricq. The 132nd and the 133rd Field Ambulances marched from here a hot and dusty way, and continental roads can be dusty in summer as muddy in winter, to the delightful retreat of Autingues, while the 134th Field Ambulance to the equally attractive and equally rustic village of Berthem.

Lieut.-Col. G. A. D. Harvey, C.M.G., arrived to take over command of the 132nd Field Ambulance on July 5th, vice Lieut.-Col. Littlejohns, and two days later the unit marched to Volkerinckove, a distance of seventeen miles, with an hour and a half rest at Estmont for refreshment. The next day another trek was accomplished and the unit arrived at Lister Camp, Rousebrugge, leaving at 5.30 a.m., and reaching their destination eighteen miles away at 3 p.m. Here the Ambulance stayed for a week, moving to Tubby Camp on the 16th, and taking over a Corps Skin Centre and D.R.S. from the 102nd Field Ambulance. Whilst here an aeroplane made a forced landing near the camp on the 29th and the observer was found to have sustained a slight flesh wound.

From Autingues, with all its pleasant associations, the 133rd Field Ambulance moved on July 7th for the Proven area, where it was to be attached to the 30th American Division. The night was spent en route at Volkerinckove, and the next day Ballance Camp was reached. Here a stay was made of some nine days, the unit moving to the II Corps Rest Station at Bollezeele on the 17th. Whilst here two memorable cricket matches were played, one on the 29th and the other on the 31st versus the A.O.D. of the Division.

The 134th Field Ambulance in like manner moved from Berthem on July 7th to join the 30th American Division, who were encamped at a point between Merkeghem and Fruckinchove. Having joined forces they moved to Nine Elms Camp, Proven, on the 9th. From here they reconnoitred the Blue Line at Poperinghe, and instructed their pupils in the possible line of evacuation.

It should be noted here that although we returned from the Base as units, yet our Division generally was not re-equipped for service as a Division but remained only at cadre strength for training purposes. When the Ambulances proceeded from the Autingues area they lost all touch with 39th D.H.Q., coming under the orders of the American Division instead. Our own D.H.Q. moved into the regions of Dieppe where they remained until after the Armistice.

August passed peacefully as far as the units were concerned. The 132nd Field Ambulance received a party from the 305th Sanitary Train for instructions on August 3rd. The Laiterie, Poperinghe was prepared for an A.D.S. on the 17th, and on the 25th the Annual Sports of the Ambulance were held, when the D.D.M.S. and the Divisional Surgeon were present. Needless to say, a most enjoyable day was spent in ideal weather. The programme consisted of some twenty events, including the usual flat and relay races, jumping, tug of war and a fancy dress parade!

It was, of course, to a different atmosphere that we returned to the Poperinghe area. The tide of war had carried the enemy to within grasping distance of this little town, and not many of its old inhabitants were left. Many of the houses and buildings had been destroyed and Talbot House had even found it necessary to evacuate its hostelry in favour of a cramped building at Proven. The genial host, however, continued his open door, and bore with him the traditions of the old home. Some can recall a Sunday at Evensong with the Padre attired in surplice, wandering about the museum-like room, reciting prayers and looking for something he had mislaid!

The 133rd Field Ambulance still remained at their ideal camp at Bollezeele, where they enjoyed some five weeks of high summer. On the 1st of the month they received a visit from the band of the East Surrey Regiment, which was much appreciated. The 10th saw another cricket match and a week

later, amid much regret, the Ambulance handed
over the Camp to the 103rd Field Ambulance.
This done the 133rd Field Ambulance marched out
to Bowlby Camp, Proven, where they took over a
M.D.S. from the 99th Field Ambulance. The
journey to Proven was a distinctly pleasant one,
through the harvest fields of this flat but attractive
area of Flanders. An ancient country still retaining
its air of old worldness and charm in spite of war
and all its madness. Not long, however, were
they destined to be at Bowlby Camp, for on the
21st, they again marched to Zermezeele, another
delightful trek to a secluded country retreat. On
the 23rd they again moved, this time making for
Arneke where they took over the XIX
Corps Rest Station from the 2/1st East Lancashire
Field Ambulance situated in a large school building
in the middle of the village. A week here, however,
and they were off again, this time to the
Second Army Dysentery Centre at Hilhoek.

The 134th Field Ambulance commenced the month
of August with a distinctly new move by laying out
on the ground adjacent to their camp a large Red
Cross some 77 feet in length, in order to designate
their unit and its purpose to enemy aircraft. This
was the first note of any such activity and is a
witness to the fact, which all our men accepted,
that the Germans played the game as far as we
were concerned and were only too sorry when
any untoward event occurred involving the medical
services. On August 16th, Major R. C. Cooke
was sent in command of an advance party to the
old and tried area adjacent to Ypres and on the

next day the Headquarters of the unit proceeded to Moor Park, South of Ypres, with the 30th American Division. It is interesting in the light of our earlier acquaintance with this part of the line to mention the location of the various posts that the 134th were now called upon to man. They show how much ground we had lost since those earlier days. The R.A.P's were at the Dolls' House, and Swan Chateau, the Relay Post at Ambulance Farm and Brandhoek. The A.D.S. at Belgian Battery Corner, with a Bearer Post at the Mill, Vlamertinghe. The Reserve A.D.S. and Field Ambulance Headquarters at Moor Park. The A.D.S. for the Green Line was at Harrison Post and the M.D.S. at Mendinghem. On the 21st the O.C. of the Ambulance inspected the various posts, including the one at Poperinghe Town Hall and the one on the outskirts of Poperinghe. It was reported on the 31st August that the enemy had retired from Kemmel Hill and accordingly, the next day being the 1st September, the R.A.P. was moved forward to Woodcote House, which had been the A.D.S. when we were in the area previously. The following letter was later received in connection with this:

"American Expeditionary Force,
September 4, 1918.
From Commanding Officer, Ambulance Co. 119, 105th Sanitary Train.

To Commanding General, 30th Division, A.E.F.

1. Following our conversation of a few days ago, it has been my pleasure to secure for you the names of the four British enlisted men who were such a

great help to us during the early morning hours of
August 27th, 1918, at Belgian Battery Corner, A.D.S.

2. 64337 Sergt. J. Nutter.
    72247 Sergt. F. G. Unwin.
    88690 L/Corpl. I. G. Millward.
    88054 Private J. R. Lawson.

The above four men are members of the R.A.M.C.
and were assigned to us by the C.O. of the 134th Field
Ambulance (British) as instructors to our enlisted men.

3. Sergts. Nutter and Unwin assisted by one
Medical Department Sergeant (American), supervised the evacuation of wounded and gas patients
from the forward area to the A.D.S., each of them
being placed in command of a group of reserve
stretcher bearers, and assigned to one of the R.A.P's
during the emergency. L/Corpl. Millward ably
supervised our force of enlisted men assigned to the
Dressing Room on this occasion, and Private
Lawson was so careful and energetic in superin-
tending the making of all necessary records that
even in the rush accuracy was maintained.

To these men, with their experience of several
years in the War Zone, the rush of patients that
followed our gas attack was not an unusual occurrence, but it was the first experience of this kind
which these American soldiers had undergone.
The calm and efficient work of these British enlisted
men did much to prevent unnecessary excitement
and gave self confidence to our men when they
were called on to meet this emergency.

(Signed) Julius A. Johnson,
1st Lieut., M.C., U.S.A."

September saw the units bid a definite farewell to Proven and the Salient. Not long was Ypres destined to trouble men's bodies and souls, but we were certainly to see it no more except as visitors in the piping times of peace seeking to perpetuate the memory of old far-off forgotten things, by means of specimen trenches and souvenirs. The 134th Field Ambulance left the line work on September 3rd and moved to Nine Elms Camp and on the next night in an endeavour to shake off the memory of mud and blood, a concert was arranged and given by the men of the unit. It needs no imagination on the part of those who were not present to state that this was a right-down good show, and in the language descriptive of such occasions, brought down the house more than once. September 6th saw the unit march to Ballance Camp, Mendinghem, whilst the next day they proceeded to Heidebeek, where they entrained for a slow and uncomfortable journey to the Somme area once more.

In sympathy with these movements the 132nd Field Ambulance handed over their D.R.S. to the 107th Field Ambulance and marched to Ballance Camp on September 3rd, entraining at Proven on the 7th. In like manner the 133rd Field Ambulance handed over their duties and responsibilities to the 138th Field Ambulance on the 4th and entrained at Heidebeek the next day.

A day and a night in the train, travelling in cattle trucks with our legs dangling over the open doorway brushing the tops of the weeds with our army boots, the plain of Flanders gave place to

the plain of Picardy and we talked and laughed
as the hours sped faster than the train. Some
played chess, other cards, while many sought to
assuage the ravages of the inner man. We talked
of the War, its prospects or otherwise of bringing
peace and what we should do when we returned
to civil life. But there was not one in those three
train loads who thought the world's ambition would
be realised so soon !

The 132nd Field Ambulance arrived at Wavrans
on the 7th, where they detrained and marched to
Hernicourt, where they came under the I
Corps, First Army. The 133rd Field Ambulance
detrained at Candas at 3 a.m. the day previously
and marched as day was breaking to Beauval.
Whilst the 134th Field Ambulance detrained at
Petit Houvin on the 8th and marched to Mesnil
St. Pol where they were billeted in an old farm.
September 14th the 132nd Field Ambulance held
a paper chase over a track of four miles, which was
thoroughly enjoyed by those who took part. On
the 18th the unit again entrained at Wavrans and
proceeded to Belle Eglise which they reached at
1.15 p.m. Here they were met by a guide who
conducted them to Louvencourt. Four days here,
however, and the unit was conveyed by 'bus to
the Tincourt area where they took over a Field
Ambulance site at Buire from the 1st Australian
Field Ambulance and a gas centre. An A.D.S.
at Hervilly was also taken over. On the 26th
September the Ambulance opened a Divisional
Walking Wounded Post at Templeux and a gas

centre at Marquaix, whilst the next day the Headquarters of the Ambulance also moved to Marquaix.
September 8th saw the 133rd Field Ambulance
march to Orville where they stayed for a fortnight,
making excursions into Doullens as opportunity
permitted, and were generally kept out of mischief
by drills, route marches and such fatigues as are
common to medical units. On the 23rd the
Ambulance entrained at Doullens and proceeded
to Tincourt which they reached about midnight.
This was an interesting journey to everyone concerned, through Amiens, Villers Brettoneaux and
the land of our recent adventures during the Retreat.
From Chaunes to Tincourt was nothing short of
appalling, the train running a few yards and then
stopping owing to the conditions of the line. The
devastation of this area was complete and filled
the brightest with feelings of gloom. One spot
we passed was labelled Misery and seemed to
speak the profoundest truth. The Germans had
been but lately driven from their short-lived gains,
but not before they had added gloom to desolation.
Arrived at Tincourt, on a perfectly moonlit night,
the unit was followed on its march to Driencourt
through the early hours of the morning by enemy
aeroplanes. From this latter place 1 officer and
71 O.R's were sent to report to Major Cranston
at Longavesnes where they remained until the
27th. On the 29th Major Warwick with 3 officers
and 108 O.R's were sent to Ronsoy to assist in the
evacuation of the line during the attack on the
famous Hindenburg Line. The party proceeded by
lorry to the strains of " The Parson's waiting for

me and my girl," to St. Emile, from whence they marched to their destination which they reached at Zero minus one hour, arriving at the gun positions just as the preliminary bombardment opened. The journey along the road was somewhat exciting as the enemy was searching the roads with gas shells, and the first obstacle passed was a G.S. wagon knocked out by the roadside. Both horses were killed and the driver, flung from his seat, lying dead at the rear.

The Ambulance was, of course, attached to the American Division and spent the next two days carrying and assisting at the various posts. At one time a congestion of badly wounded cases occurred in the yard of some shattered buildings as there was some difficulty in evacuation owing to a difference of pattern between the American cars and our stretchers. The enemy started retaliation with high explosive shells and it was nothing short of a miracle that these fell on the other side of the road to where the poor fellows, both English, American and German were lying helpless and we helpless to assist them. One shell in the vicinity and many would have been beyond ultimate human aid. During these operations, Lieut. D. G. K. Garrett, a Canadian Officer attached to the 133rd, was killed in action. October 1st saw the Division relieved and we accordingly returned to Driencourt.

The 134th Field Ambulance had their portion of the line during the month of September and on the 17th they entrained at Petit Houvain en route for Lealvillers where they were billeted in barns. A few days later, on the 23rd, the personnel were

taken by 'bus to Brusle, and on the 25th, the unit
marched to Hervilly, from whence an A.D.S. was
taken over at Jeancourt. Major R. C. Cooke and
Major J. H. Porter proceeded to take over the
various forward posts from the 118th Australian
Field Ambulance. Zero hour on the 29th found
this Ambulance in readiness and although appalling
weather set in with all its contingent mud and
slush, wounded came through in a constant stream
all day and were evacuated without a hitch. A
large number of German prisoners were taken and
used for the evacuation of the wounded. As a contrast
to all our previous experience this was now a war
of progression and when the Ambulance moved
forward to Asservillers on October 2nd and eventually marched out of the line, they handed all the
surplus equipment to the Australians, but the
A.D.S. was not included as this was too far in the
rear. For the work which he carried out in the
forward area during this operation, Major R. C.
Cooke was awarded the D.S.O.

October was a sad month for the 132nd Field
Ambulance. On the 2nd they closed the gas
centre at Marquaix and marched to Biaches. Whilst
on the 5th the unit proceeded by 'bus to Templeux
le Guerard from whence the next day it took over
the evacuation of the forward area from the 6th
Australian Field Ambulance, establishing themselves in the quarries of this desolate area with
A.D.S. at Estrees. The next day Major Morris,
second in command, was killed, his head being
blown off by a shell, whilst visiting an R.A.P.
at Diamler Post. A death that was sorely lamented,

not only by the personnel of the 132nd but the other Ambulances as well. Major Morris had identified himself with the fortunes of his Ambulance for so long that it was difficult to imagine the unit without him.

The 117th and 118th American Infantry Regiments attacked at 5.10 a.m., October 8th, and gained all their objectives. So much so that the next day after the Division had again attacked at dawn, the 132nd Field Ambulance received orders to advance their A.D.S. to Geneve in the Montbrehain area, and a school which had been used as a German hospital was taken over. The 119th Field Ambulance relieved the 132nd Field Ambulance of the site at Montbrehain on the 10th, establishing a M.D.S. and Gas Centre there. Accordingly the unit moved to Busigny. On the 12th the 132nd handed over its A.D.S. and the various posts of the forward area to the 106th Sanitary Train and returned to Montbrehain. The 17th saw a M.D.S. established at Bohain in a large factory by this Ambulance and on the 19th, 1 N.C.O. and 1 man were wounded near Molain. On the 21st the unit marched to a quarry near Bellicourt where it spent the night. Before leaving here, the next morning, the Ambulance paid its last tribute of respect to their dead officer, parading round the grave where the Last Post was sounded. This done the Ambulance proceeded to Marquaix where it entrained and proceeded to Bonnay. Here uncertainty arose as to where the Ambulance was to go as no definite orders could be obtained, with the result that they marched to Bazieux and

Contay, finally settling at the Chateau at Vadencourt where a Camp Infirmary or Hospital was established on the 23rd. The next day the main body of the Ambulance arrived having detrained at Albert, marching the eight and a half miles from there.

The 134th Field Ambulance said goodbye to Major J. H. Porter on the 3rd October, on his being transferred to the 81st Wing, R.A.F. Major Porter had been with the Ambulance and also engaged on staff work with the A.D.M.S. at D.H.Q., for a very long time, his parting, therefore, was looked upon with regret.

Major R. C. Cooke now assumed temporary command of the Ambulance during the absence of the O.C. on leave. The next day the unit marched to Hamel to a hospital under canvas, except a bearer sub-division which was moved by 'bus to Ronsoy in preparation for another attack. The 6th saw the Ambulance proceed to Templeux, where the transport was left, whilst the main body marched on to Hargicourt where they took over a Walking Wounded Post from the 7th Australian Field Ambulance. From here, the next day, they moved to Bellicourt and had the onerous duty of supervising the despatch of a train-load of civilians from the danger zone back to Tincourt. Zero hour was at 5.10 the next morning, and the attack succeeded beyond all expectations, the Hindenberg Line was indeed broken and the movements in consequence were rapid. The G.O.C. Fourth Army inspected the camp during the day and noted the system of evacuation which was by lorry and light railway. The next day a move forward was made to Joncourt, where a Walking Wounded Centre was established. It was the case now of establishing a position in the morning which was hopelessly out of touch with events at night. German retaliation by artillery fire was becoming less and less, and we were marching on to villages occupied by civilians that had been under the German regime for so long a time. Too often we were finding children in the firing line, and civilians, who had to be provided for and protected against gas attacks and as speedily as possible evacuated. The marches were a slow progress through the entanglements of the fortresses of the Hindenberg Line, but once through the way was easier and we came upon little gardens that yielded us fresh vegetables for the eternal stew. On one occasion we saw some nurses who had evidently come up to see what they could. They were certainly much farther forward than they should have been, but realising they were something of a gazing stock they soon jumped off the lorry in which they were riding and made their way back. Bellicourt and its district was full of interest when the shells had ceased to fall and provided us with a good deal of sight-seeing. The village itself was built over the Cambrai—St. Quentin Canal, the waters of which ran below by means of a tunnel. The enemy had made good use of this underground waterway, the tunnel providing a natural and capacious shelter for battalions of his men. Access was gained by one or two saps that led down from the ground floor of the ruined houses above.

It was a somewhat eerie sensation to be apparently descending into the bowels of the earth and to suddenly find oneself on the shore of the dark waters and see the outlines of huge barges moored in what looked like the waters of Charon. The barges had been fitted up with electric light and bunks and were the billets of the waiting German troops. At the entrance to the Canal, in the rooms where once the lock keeper worked, were very excellent soup kitchens that had been used to provide the enemy troops in the trenches with hot meals. The soup kitchens, containing as they did the fatty remains of former stews apparently gave rise to the wild rumours that had sprung up concerning the melting down of bodies in order to obtain fat. We had been assured that this tunnel was the very place where it had been carried out, but the soup tureens remained the only tangible evidence. So much for this and other tales of horror with which we were fed daily during the period of the War.

When the canal left the tunnel and passed on through the steep banks towards St. Quentin it was a matter for poetic reflection as to the beauty of its strangely irridescent water. The South bank, or the one nearest our old line, was a fine sight with its mass of bushes now turned into autumn gold, whilst the North bank, or the one which had borne the brunt of our bombardment was a sight of torn and blasted barrenness. It must have been a tremendous piece of heroism that floated our men across the intervening water in order to scale and capture the stronghold on the other side. The lifebelts they used were still floating about as flotsam in the sluggish tide.

Joncourt was handed over to the 27th American Division on the 12th October and the unit proceeded to Brancourt, whilst on the 15th a Walking Wounded Centre was established on the Busigny—Vaux Andigny Road. A loading post was also established at Montbrehain Railhead. Zero hour struck again at 5.20 on October 17th, and the next day the Walking Wounded Station was moved to Vaux Andigny. On the 20th the Ambulance moved to Busigny from whence, all unwittingly, they said goodbye to line work and marched back to Estrees on the 21st to Marquaix on the 22nd and to Tincourt on the 23rd. At this point the Ambulance entrained, the transport moving to Roisel for the same purpose. The 24th saw the unit arrive at Heilly from whence they marched to Warloy.

October 2nd, saw the 133rd Field Ambulance march to Courcelles where they were billeted in huts. The next day a billeting party was sent to Suzanne where they proceeded to make themselves comfortable for the night on discarded spring mattresses. These beds had been but lately used by the German troops who had evidently removed them from the fine old chateau adjacent. Plans, however, were soon changed and this party returned to Headquarters through Peronne. On the 8th, the unit moved to Templeux le Guerard where they spent the night in tents. The next day saw them march on through the Hindenberg Line to Wiancourt, an interesting, though fatiguing journey, owing to the congested nature of the road. Dead horses, dead men, friend and foe, were lying on every hand, many of the enemy dead having lain there for many a day until index bones were protruding from index fingers. A dead German sniper had toppled out of the tree from which he had been sniping, when caught by one of our bullets, and lay in the orchard as he had fallen, beside the billet where the Ambulance slept that night. The next day saw more advancing and the unit marched to Premont where they slept in tents by the side of a field. Nearby was a German cemetery with its large concrete cross and well kept little graves all decked with autumn flowers. The way to this halting place was difficult as the cross roads in most cases had been mined, resulting in huge craters that necessitated wide detours. The German artillery was faintly but persistently shelling the two villages, resulting in not much of damage. The Ambulance remained at Premont for a day or two.

Some men were sent up to Busigny and had the novel experience of finding civilians in the same area as the A.D.S., which was not in a ruined village as we had become accustomed to, but a place that had only been damaged by desultory fighting. The men, however, were moved back some mile and a half to a large farm where they awaited orders. On the 16th the personnel again moved up to Busigny where they took over some small houses for the work, the floors of which were littered with the little treasures of the recent owners. The next day, being the 17th, an A.D.S. was opened at Estcaufort and the personnel were taken up by char-a-bancs. A constant stream of wounded came through all day, including a good many German lightly wounded. The A.D.S. was in a large house, some treasures of which still remained. The next day the guns were moved forward and our work began to slacken off. On this day the transport moved up to Busigny and on the way had the unpleasant experience of a bomb accidentally exploding, wounding two men and three horses; one horse so badly that it died. The next day saw the A.D.S. at Estcaufort closed and a new one opened at St. Souplet. Here the Ambulance sustained casualties in 4 O.R. wounded and 16 O.R. gassed. This was to be the unit's last experience of the line and one of the last cases was that of a gunner brought in from one of the heavy batteries nearby. A shell had lit just in front of the guns, wounding several and shattering this poor man's legs. As the doctor was amputating the remnants the man suddenly asked what he was doing. The officer replied that he was just tidying up his legs. The man was evacuated cheerful enough, but died soon afterwards from shock. Whilst in this district, too, the Ambulance had to provide funeral parties for some civilians who had been killed by a shell that burst in their house.

The 21st saw the Ambulance moving back by long marches to a place of rest, and Brancourt was reached where the night was spent. This was, of course, erstwhile German territory and there was a general scare of delayed mines. The church here was given the benefit of the doubt and left severely alone. The next morning the unit was off again marching through Mont Brehain, Estrees, Nauroy, to that scene of utter desolation, Bellicourt, where the night was spent in some old saps. The 23rd was another day of marching, through Hargicourt and Roisel to Marquaix where the night of wind and cold was spent. The day following the unit marched back to Roisel to entrain, which feat was accomplished after a long and tedious wait at 3 p.m. Corbie sur Somme was reached at midnight, after the usual slow and jogging progress, and the Ambulance marched to billets in a row of little cottages down a very deserted street. The twin towers of Corbie Church rose up amid the fields, battered, it is true, by that recent tide, but worthy of the name and dignity of Abbey.

Influenza was now rampant amongst the troops and quite a number of our men fell victims. One Sergeant of the 133rd, M. T. Mills, a man of delightful personality, died.

We were now, the three Ambulances, concentrated in the Somme area and but little work fell to our lot. We took walks about the open country and watched our Army's effort at cultivation of the soil. Walked along the banks of old Somme, that could be beautiful in autumn as in spring, and discussed, amid the falling leaves, the prospects of this and that. Noticed the quiet hand of Mother Earth covering over her wounds in peaceful persistency and in one case the elfin sight of a whole field covered with gossamer threads spun as by magic, with the silken cords catching the light. Some made excursions into Amiens and walked along the quiet streets, visited the cathedral and saw as much as sandbags would allow. But what the sandbags could not hide we enjoyed, of noble proportions and Gothic thought. One or two shells had pierced the lofty roof but seemed to have done but little damage. There was Villers Brettoneaux, too, which some remembered as a peaceful retreat of little houses, ivy clad, serene and lovely. Now, alas, a heap of unutterable desolation with the graves of many Australians lining the railway.

Went into Albert and noticed the Basilica had lost its leaning Madonna and Child and recalled the legends which had grown about this famous tower. Whilst some still cherish the memory of walks made under the pale and spreading light of the Hunters' Moon along those white roads from Corbie to Villers Brettoneaux.

But, generally, we made ourselves comfortable, ate as much food as we could get and foraged for fuel. One unit discovered the proximity of a large stock of wine barrels, empty, of course. In but a few days those oaken staves had been turned into the silk of white ash on the open hearths of those little houses, and one man, who sat too close, had the backs of his hands blistered by the cheerful flames. One sad duty befell the 134th Field Ambulance when Sergt. Heathfield, A.S.C.M.T., who had died of pneumonia on November 3rd, was buried on November 4th, at Warloy.

And then the rumours of War began to trickle through. First came the Surrender of Turkey, then Austria, and finally that Germany had sent delegates to meet Marshal Foch, resulting in the signing of the Armistice at 11 a.m., on November 11th.

Armistice Day was celebrated very quietly. We were, of course, with American rather than our own troops and many miles behind any scene of strife. The refugees had trickled back to these ruined areas in which we now were, and it was surprising how many national flags were instantly mustered and fluttered feebly here and there. Shattered churches with perhaps one bell in the steeple, found willing hands to ring that solo peal, hours on end, *ad nauseum*, to express a great joy and an infinite relief.

We remained in our respective locations some few days longer, but our fate was now definitely sealed. On the 14th November at 10 a.m., the 132nd Field Ambulance took part in an inspection and march past of the whole Division by the Divisional Commander. The 134th Field Ambulance had the pleasure of placing on record that many of their men had been cited in the 30th American Divisional Orders of November 2nd, for meritorious conduct during the operations of September 29th to October 19th. These were:—

Temp. Capt. A/Major R. C. Cooke, M.C.
Capt. and Q.M. E. G. Floyd.
72274 Sergt. F. W. Unwin.
M2/074752 Cpl. A/Sergt. S. Heathfield.
72277 Cpl. A/Sergt. E. A. Cradduck.
72169 Cpl. W. C. Daniels, M.M.
T4/065479 Dr. G. Bowers.
42824 Private A. R. Sim.
M2/021134 Private T. H. Bayliss
1237 Private W. Hellier.
72245 Private W. J. Gallagher.
M1/08743 Private T. H. Thompson.

On the 17th November the 132nd and the 134th Field Ambulance marched to Picquigny, the next day marching on to Abbeville. Whilst on the 18th the whole of the 133rd Personnel were taken by lorry to Abbeville also, where a stay of some days was made in bell tents. Whilst here, on November 19th, the 134th Field Ambulance received the welcome news that the M.M. had been conferred on the following.

> 72274   Sergt. F. W. Unwin.
> 42824   Private A. R. Sim.
> 72245   Private W. J. Gallagher.
> M2/074752   Cpl. A/Sergt. S. Heathfield
> (posthumous)
> M1/08743   Private T. H. Thompson.

It was of a different Abbeville we now made acquaintance. Whereas before it was dead and deserted, now all was life and light with open shops and a gay array of illuminations about the streets. Here the three units once more handed in their equipment, said goodbye to horses and wagons, especially the wheels thereof, and on the 9th December proceeded to Etaples where they were definitely disbanded. Goodbyes were again said, this time more cheerfully, and in twos and threes were posted to other units and other Divisions. Many in due time finding their way to Cologne before returning to civil life and the cares which they never thought before could possibly exist.

The following despatches which were received by the units concerned speak for themselves and form a fitting conclusion to our work.

" Headquarters, 30th Division,
American E.F.
November 4th, 1918.

From: The Divisional Surgeon.

To: The D.G.M.S., B.E.F., France
(through the Corps Surgeon, II American Corps)

Subject: British Field Ambulances, Nos. 132 and
134.

1. The Divisional Surgeon desires to express appreciation of the services of the British Field Ambulances (Nos. 132 and 134), which were attached to this Division from July 6th, 1918, to November 18, 1918. During the months of July and August this Division was under active training and the British Ambulances assisted materially in the case of the sick and in the training of the Sanitary units of the Division. The American equipment and methods of supply were replaced by British, and the assistance given by the British units at this period was considerable. During the period of active operations against the enemy, the British Field Ambulances were utilised in the evacuation of wounded in conjunction with the American Field Ambulances. At all times the character of the work was of the highest and co-operation between the American and British units was notable. That the Field of battle was continuously cleared, that many thousands were evacuated, and that there was no record of delay in evacuation, speaks for itself.

Efficiency, co-operation and capacity for unlimited work made it possible to care for casualties in an expeditious and effective manner. The Field Ambulances concerned are to be given the highest praise for the work performed.

2. The organisation and discipline of the 132nd and 134th Field Ambulances is excellent. Devotion to duty and loyalty to superiors on the part of both officer and enlisted personnel was noted on all occasions. The Division Surgeon desires to express again his appreciation of the loyalty, ability and efficiency of Field Ambulances Nos. 132 and 134.

(Signed) A. M. Whaley,
Colonel, Medical Corps, U.S.A."

" D.G.M.S.

In forwarding the foregoing, I desire to add my appreciation of the services rendered by the 132nd and 134th British Field Ambulance Companies as well as the 133rd Field Ambulance Company which were attached to this Corps during our stay in the British area.

(Signed) C. C. Collins,
Colonel, Medical Corps, U.S.A.

Office of the Corps Surgeon,
Headquarters, II Corps,
A.E.F., 3rd December, 1918."

DECORATIONS

C.B.

Colonel G. W. BRAZIER-CREAGH,
    C.M.G. (4/6/17)   A.D.M.S., 39th Division

D.S.O.

Lieut-Colonel H. C. HILDRETH	O.C., 134th Field Ambulance
Lieut.-Colonel A. S. LITTLEJOHNS	O.C., 132nd Field Ambulance
Major C. R. MILLAR	D.A.D.M.S., 39th Division
Major J. S. Y. ROGERS (*wounded*)	M.O. i/c 4/5th Black Watch
Captain A. S. WILLIAMS	O.C., 133rd Field Ambulance
Captain E. H. MOORE	M.O. i/c 11th Royal Sussex
Lieut.-Colonel S. MILLER, M.C.	O.C., 133rd Field Ambulance
Major R. C. COOKE, M.C.	134th Field Ambulance

BAR to D.S.O.

Major J. S. Y. ROGERS (*wounded*)   M.O. i/c 4/5th Black Watch

MILITARY CROSS

Captain C. F. HACKER	M.O. i/c 1st Herts. Regiment
Captain R. I. HARRIS (*wounded*)	134th Field Ambulance
Captain S. MILLER	132nd Field Ambulance
Captain J. MORRIS (*Killed*)	132nd Field Ambulance
Captain L. R. MEECH (*wounded*)	133rd Field Ambulance
Lieutenant J. B. DUNNING (*wounded*)	M.O. i/c 13th Royal Sussex
Lieutenant S. J. DARKE (*wounded*)	M.O. i/c 16th Rifle Brigade
Lieutenant J. W. WAYTE (*wounded*)	M.O. i/c 14th Hants Regiment
Captain W. T. BROWN (*wounded*)	M.O. i/c 13th Gloucester Regt.
Captain H. J. de BRENT (*wounded*)	M.O. i/c 6th Cheshires
Captain J. P. CHARLES (*wounded*)	M.O. i/c 1st Herts Regiment
Captain J. H. C. GATCHELL (*killed*)	M.O. i/c 11th Royal Sussex
Captain D. J. MACDOUGALL (*wounded*)	M.O. i/c 13th Royal Sussex
Captain H. D. H. WILLIS-BUND	M.O. i/c 1st Cambs.
Captain J. H. PORTER	134th Field Ambulance
Captain A. E. KNIGHT	D.A.D.M.S., 39th Division
Captain R. C. COOKE	M.O. i/c 17th Sherwoods
Captain H. F. WARWICK (*wounded*)	133rd Field Ambulance
Captain S. J. L. LINDEMAN	M.O. i/c 16th Sherwoods
Lieutenant D. J. VALENTINE	M.O. i/c 11th Royal Sussex
Lieutenant J. B. CLINTON, M.O.R.C., U.S.A.	M.O. i/c 1st Cambs.
Lieutenant G. H. BOYER, M.O.R.C., U.S.A.	133rd Field Ambulance

BAR to MILITARY CROSS
Captain R. I. HARRIS (*wounded*)   134th Field Ambulance
Captain W. T. BROWN (*wounded*) 132nd Field Ambulance

MENTIONED IN DESPATCHES
Colonel G. W. BRAZIER-CREAGH,
    C.B., C.M.G. (Three times)   A.D.M.S., 39th Div.
Captain G. D. ROBERTSON   133rd Field Ambulance
Captain C. H. LILLEY (*wounded*)   O.C., 82nd Sanitary Section
Lieut.-Colonel H. C. HILDRETH   O.C., 134th Field Ambulance
Lieut.-Colonel A. S. LITTLEJOHNS O.C., 132nd Field Ambulance
Captain J. H. PORTER   134th Field Ambulance
Captain W. T. BROWN   M.O. i/c 13th Gloucesters
Captain R. C. COOKE   M.O. i/c 17th Sherwoods
Captain G. H. HUGGINS   134th Field Ambulance
Captain A. E. DELGADO (*wounded*) M.O. i/c 186th Brigade R.F.A.
Captain J. S. MANFORD   O.C., 133rd Field Ambulance
Major J. S. Y. ROGERS, D.S.O.
              (*wounded*)   M.O. i/c 4/5th Black Watch
Captain E. BOYERS   M.O. i/c 17th K.R.R.C.
Captain C. D. COYLE (*wounded*) M.O. i/c 14th Hants Regiment
Captain A. W. DENNIS   M.O. i/c 16th Rifle Brigade
Captain S. J. L. LINDEMAN   M.O. i/c 16th Sherwoods
Lieutenant & Q.M. C. W. AUDUS 133rd Field Ambulance

CROIX DE GUERRE (With Palm)
Major J. S. Y. ROGERS, D.S.O.
              (*wounded*) M.O. i/c 4/5th Black Watch

D.C.M.
No.
  72297 S/Sergt. SANDERS, C.   134th Field Ambulance
  72320 Private A/Corpl. TALLON, H. 134th Field Ambulance
  39169 S/Sergt. WILLIAMS, O. T. 133rd Field Ambulance
M2/132876 Sergt. PEEL, H. F.   A.S.C., M.T., attached
                           133rd Field Ambulance

MILITARY MEDALS
No.
  44157 Private MEREDITH, S.   133rd Field Ambulance
  88053 Private KEPPY, V. H.   133rd Field Ambulance
  65775 Sergt. LOAKES, F. W.   132nd Field Ambulance
  63252 Private MARSTON, J. L. I. 133rd Field Ambulance
  65938 Sergt. EARL, C.   133rd Field Ambulance
  65994 Private EUSTACE, T.   133rd Field Ambulance
  72277 Private A/Sergt. CRADDUCK,
                 E. A. 134th Field Ambulance
  45012 Private BRADLEY, J. H.   134th Field Ambulance
  72130 Private TAYLOR, T.   134th Field Ambulance
  74443 Private A/Sergt. SEARLE, C. H. 134th Field Ambulance
  72169 Private DANIELS, W. C.   134th Field Ambulance
  65893 Sergt. DINSDALE, R.   132nd Field Ambulance

Military Medals—*contd.*

69659	Private FRANCIS, H. T.	132nd Field Ambulance
65867	Private EVERALL, H.	132nd Field Ambulance
72773	Private HARTWELL, O.	132nd Field Ambulance
72003	Private HODSON, F.	133rd Field Ambulance
77444	Private HODGSON, F.	133rd Field Ambulance
93945	Sergt. MITCHELSON, P. J.	133rd Field Ambulance
65863	S/Sergt. HODGES, F. A.	132nd Field Ambulance
65868	Private DANIELS, W.	132nd Field Ambulance
65884	L/Corpl. FAIRBROTHER, F. T.	132nd Field Ambulance
44330	Private CULLEN, J.	134th Field Ambulance
65812	Corporal MANN, F. H.	132nd Field Ambulance
72117	Private GREEN, A.	133rd Field Ambulance
65792	Sergeant REEVE, A. G.	132nd Field Ambulance
65880	Private STEVENS, E.	132nd Field Ambulance
72040	Private WEBB, A. L.	132nd Field Ambulance
65924	Private ABRAHAM, J.	132nd Field Ambulance
65772	Private NEALE, H. C.	132nd Field Ambulance
82054	Private KING, H.	132nd Field Ambulance
55621	Private HOBSON, T. H.	132nd Field Ambulance
72105	Private CLIPSON, F. W.	133rd Field Ambulance
72068	Private POWELL, G.	133rd Field Ambulance
42441	Private GROVES, G. A.	133rd Field Ambulance
72102	Private RUNHAM, H. A.	133rd Field Ambulance
42357	Private KENNEDY, C.	133rd Field Ambulance
64337	Sergeant NUTTER, J. B.	134th Field Ambulance
3301	Private ARRIGHO, R.	134th Field Ambulance
73365	Private BROOKES, W. J.	134th Field Ambulance
46336	Private TAYLOR, A. J.	134th Field Ambulance
52777	Private MELLOR, A.	134th Field Ambulance
M2/147314	Private CRAIGS, R. L.	A.S.C., M.T., attached 134th Field Ambulance
M2/132732	Private KAY, D. C.	A.S.C., M.T., attached 132nd Field Ambulance
C/1030	Sergeant STINCHCOMBE, E. S.	A.S.C., M.T., attached 132nd Field Ambulance
M2/132136	Private COUSINS, M.	A.S.C., M.T., attached 133rd Field Ambulance
M2/132247	Private CONNOR, C.	A.S.C., M.T., attached 133rd Field Ambulance
59012	Sergeant WISHART, D. G.	133rd Field Ambulance
M2/073142	Private ABBOTT, W. W.	A.S.C., M.T., attached 134th Field Ambulance
M2/132740	Private LASCELLES, K. W.	A.S.C., M.T., attached 134th Field Ambulance
72274	Sergeant Unwin, F. W.	134th Field Ambulance
42824	Private Sim, A. R.	134th Field Ambulance
72245	Private Gallagher, W. J.	134th Field Ambulance
M2/074752	Corpl. A/Sergt. HEATHFIELD, S. (*Posthumous*)	134th Field Ambulance
M1/08743	Private THOMPSON, T. H.	134th Field Ambulance

BRONZE MEDAL FOR VALOUR

No.
65867 Private EVERALL, H.   132nd Field Ambulance

BELGIAN CROIX DE GUERRE

No.
88503 Private KEMP, G.   133rd Field Ambulance
46092 Private KIRKHAM, S. W.   134th Field Ambulance

MERITORIOUS SERVICE MEDAL

No.
35954 Sergt.-Major ROBERTSON, D.
                         C. S.   134th Field Ambulance
72241 Sergt.-Major HERBERT, F. G.   133rd Field Ambulance
72152 Sergt. A/Q.M.S. HERBERT, F. H. A.D.M.S. Office
65795 Sergeant PIPER, A. C.   132nd Field Ambulance

MENTIONED IN DESPATCHES

No.
38943 Sergt.-Major SHARPE, B. G.   132nd Field Ambulance
57252 Private DYE, H.   133rd Field Ambulance
65965 Private STREDWICK, J.   133rd Field Ambulance
C/1030 Sergeant STINCHCOMBE, E. S. A.S.C., M.T., attached
                                              132nd Field Ambulance

GLOSSARY

A.D.S.	... ...	Advanced Dressing Station.
A.D.V.S.	... ...	Assistant Director of Veterinary Services.
A.F.A.	... ...	Army Field Artillery.
A.O.D.	... ...	Army Ordnance Department.
A.D.M.S.	... ...	Assistant Director of Medical Services.
B.H.Q.	... ...	Brigade or Battalion Head Quarters.
C.C.S. ...	... ...	Casualty Clearing Station.
C.R.S. ...	... ...	Corps Rest Station.
C.R.A.	... ...	Commandant, Royal Artillery.
C.R.E. ...	... ...	Commandant, Royal Engineers.
C.M.D.S.	... ...	Corps Main Dressing Station.
D.D.M.S.	... ...	Deputy Director Medical Services (Corps).
D.A.D.M.S. ...	...	Deputy Assistant Director Medical Services.
D.R.S. ...	... ...	Divisional Rest Station.
D.C.P....	... ...	Divisional Collecting Post.
D.A.C.	... ...	Divisional Ammunition Column.
D.H.Q.	... ...	Division Head Quarters.
D.L.I. ...	... ...	Durham Light Infantry.
D.A.D.O.S. ...	...	Deputy Assistant Director Ordnance Supplies.
F.A.P. ...	... ...	Field Ambulance Post.
F.G.C.M.	... ...	Field General Court Martial.
F.A. ...	... ...	Field Ambulance.
G.O.C.	... ...	General Officer Commanding.
G.S.O....	... ...	General Staff Officer.
G.O.K.	... ...	God Only Knows.
H.Q. ...	... ...	Head Quarters.
H.T., A.S.C. ...	...	Horse Transport, Army Service Corps.
M.T., A.S.C.	...	Mechanical Transport, Army Service Corps.
M.D.S.	... ...	Main Dressing Station.
N.Y.D.	... ...	Not Yet Diagnosed.
O.P. ...	... ...	Observation Post.
O.R. ...	... ...	Other Ranks.
P.U.O....	... ...	Pyrexia, Unknown Origin.
Q. ...	... ...	Quartermaster, General Branch.
R.M.O.	... ...	Regimental Medical Officer.
R.A.P....	... ...	Regimental Aid Post.
S.M.O.	... ...	Senior Medical Officer.
T.U. ...	... ...	Temporarily Unfit.

ND - #0156 - 270225 - C0 - 198/129/15 - PB - 9781910500217 - Matt Lamination